Nature's Treasures

Written by Ben Hoare

Illustrated by Kaley McKean

Contents

MINERALS AND ROCKS

MADE BY NATURE

Introduction

Wherever we look in the world, there are natural treasures to be found.

This is a book about the many wonderful things made by animals, plants, and the Earth itself. In these pages, you will find dazzling feathers, armored fruit, extraordinary eggs, bristly teeth, leaf skeletons, glittering gems, ancient fossils, exploding seeds, super-sticky webs, rocks from outer space, and much, much more. You will discover where to find these intriguing items, how they work, and how people use them.

Every fascinating object featured tells a different story. Yet they are also connected because they are all part of the 4.5-billion-year history of life on Earth.

The variety of life is endless. The more time we spend looking at the world around us, the more we will notice and the more we will learn. Perhaps we will also become better at caring for the planet's natural treasures. After all, human beings are part of nature, too.

Ben Hoare
Author

Nature's treasures

Objects in the natural world come from a variety of places. They can be grouped according to what has made them and what they are made from. The three main types are objects that are parts of animals, plants, and minerals, such as feathers, leaves, and crystals. However, some objects are built by organisms from materials around them.

ANIMALS

Animals make up the largest category of life. So far, we have identified around two million species, most of which are insects, but there are millions more yet to be discovered. Every species is given a scientific name, often based on Latin, the language of the ancient Romans.

Zebras have hooves made from tough keratin.

Houseleeks have spirals of firm leaves that store water.

PLANTS, FUNGI, AND ALGAE

Plants form the second largest category of life. They make their own food in a process called photosynthesis. Like animals, each species has a scientific name. Some objects are made by organisms that look a lot like plants, but are actually different kinds of life—these include fungi and algae.

MINERALS AND ROCKS

Minerals are solid materials that occur naturally all over the Earth and beneath its surface. Each type of mineral is made from a different mixture of chemicals. We find some as colorful gemstones. Although they are not alive, minerals do change, and they often combine to form rocks.

These lumps of ruby are stuck inside a piece of rock.

This tubular case is home to the caddisfly larva that built it.

MADE BY NATURE

Many natural objects are not parts of living things but instead are created by animals. Nests, webs, and dung balls are all made from materials that creatures create or find in their environment. There are no plans for building these items; animals know how by instinct.

Noticing nature

Nature preserves are wonderful, but they are not the only places with wildlife and natural treasures. You can find nature in the most unexpected locations, even in towns and cities. Simply keep your eyes open. Wherever you look, you will start to make fascinating discoveries.

Beach

Park

Forest

Meadow

Where to look
You will have more success if you look up, behind, and under things, rather than just staring from a distance. Get down to ground level and explore different habitats. Beaches, parks, forests, and meadows are good places to begin searching.

When to look

Some things are best searched for during a particular season or time of day. Many fruits and seeds appear in the fall, for instance. The weather can also make a difference. Spider's webs show up when rain, fog, or dew covers them in water droplets.

Nature collections

The first natural history museums were called "cabinets of curiosities," also known by the German name "Wunderkammer." They were display cases, or sometimes entire rooms, for showing off private collections of natural treasures. Modern public museums have large collections used for education and research.

Responsible nature spotting

Although it is tempting to take the beautiful natural things you find, remember that animals and plants may still need them. An empty bird's nest, for example, may later be reused by other animals. If you leave your discoveries, other people can enjoy them, too.

Do

- Take an adult with you when you go exploring

- Dress correctly for the weather

- Make notes and take photographs of your finds

- Examine objects and then replace them

- Wash your hands after handling nests and pellets

- Close gates behind you

Don't

- Disturb wild animals, plants, or other wildlife, and never touch eggs

- Taste fruits, seeds, leaves, or anything else you find—they might be poisonous

- Touch objects unless you know they are safe

- Buy coral, shells, insects, or bones as souvenirs

- Leave litter behind

9

CHAPTER 1

Animals

Animals live in every part of the world. To help them survive in such a wide range of different habitats, they have developed an astonishing variety of body parts and structures. From the delicate beauty of the scale on a butterfly's wing to the giant grinding teeth of an elephant, there are many animal objects to marvel at.

Pointed end

This egg has one pointed end, which allows it to fit snugly with the three other eggs in the nest.

Ringed plover eggs are well camouflaged against pebbles.

Tiny holes

You can just spot the tiny holes, called pores, in this close-up view of a chicken egg. Oxygen enters the egg through these.

Spots and squiggles match the plover's nest.

Calcium carbonate is white and so are eggshells, unless other pigments are mixed in.

Bird egg

Fragile and beautiful, this wonder of nature protects the chick inside it and contains everything a baby bird needs to develop.

A bird's egg is magical to see. It is a sign of new life beginning. This pretty egg was laid by a female ringed plover in her nest on a pebble beach. Just a day earlier, it was a floppy balloon inside her body. First, the bright yellow yolk formed, then came the watery, gloopy goo called albumen, or egg white. Next, a thin membrane was added to hold it all together, and, finally, came a shell of white calcium carbonate—the same material that makes chalk. As a finishing touch, color was smeared on, and the mother plover was ready to lay her egg.

The incredible process of building an egg like this takes just 24 hours, but it uses masses of energy. Female birds need to feed up first. They eat bones or snail shells to get extra calcium to make the shell. It is worth it! Each freshly laid egg is a perfect life-support system. Safe inside, the tiny baby—at this stage called an embryo—starts out as a speck no bigger than a period, but soon it will grow into a chick.

Ringed plover
(Charadrius hiaticula)
The ringed plover breeds in the northern half of the world. It lays a clutch, or group, of four eggs in a nest on the ground.

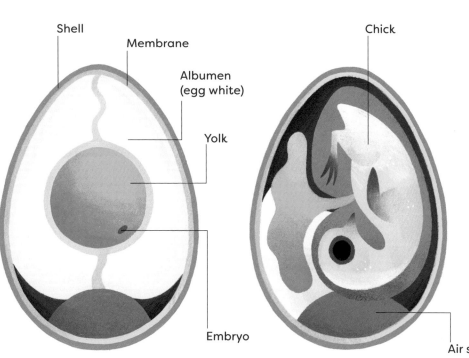

Shell

Membrane

Albumen (egg white)

Yolk

Chick

Embryo

Air store

Inside an egg
As the embryo grows, it uses up the food inside the yolk and egg white. Oxygen enters through tiny holes in the shell. When the chick is ready to hatch, it takes its first breath from the air store found at one end of the egg.

13

Bird eggs

Birds' eggs look very different, so it may come as a surprise to learn that they all get their color from just two pigments—a red-brown one and a green one. As the pigments mix, they create a wonderful variety of delicate shades and patterns.

Ruby-throated hummingbird

These pea-sized eggs weigh barely 0.02 oz (0.5 g). That may not seem like much, but they are huge compared to the 0.1 oz (3 g) female hummingbird that lays them.

Eurasian cuckoo

The female cuckoo lays her eggs in the nests of other birds, one per nest, for them to look after. To trick the host parents, her egg looks very similar to theirs.

American robin

These bright blue eggs stand out a mile. Scientists think that stronger female robins lay brighter eggs, which encourages the male robins to bring more food to their chicks.

Domestic chicken

Humans have bred hens that can lay 300 eggs a year. Their wild ancestor, the red junglefowl, lays a single clutch of five to eight eggs in the same time.

Elegant crested tinamou

Tinamou eggs are smooth and as glossy as polished gems. They can be pink or purple, green or blue. In this species, they are olive green.

Common guillemot

Each guillemot egg looks different, as if paint has been flicked at it. This helps the parents spot their egg among all the others on the cliffs where they nest.

Egg shapes

Different types of birds lay eggs of different shapes and sizes. We often think of an oval chicken egg as the typical egg shape. However, many birds lay pointed, pear-shaped, or perfectly round eggs.

Oval

Conical

Pear-shaped

Spherical

Emu

The female emu lays massive dark green or black eggs with a beautiful shine. As with ostriches, it is the male emu that looks after them.

Ostrich

At 3 lb (1.5 kg), this is the world's largest bird egg. It is white to reflect heat, so that it does not cook in the hot desert sun.

Hatching turtle

A baby loggerhead turtle breaks free from its egg after around 60 days inside. Turtles and other reptiles lay eggs quite different from those of birds. The shells are soft, white, and round. The mother usually buries her eggs in warm sand or vegetation to incubate the babies inside, helping them grow.

17

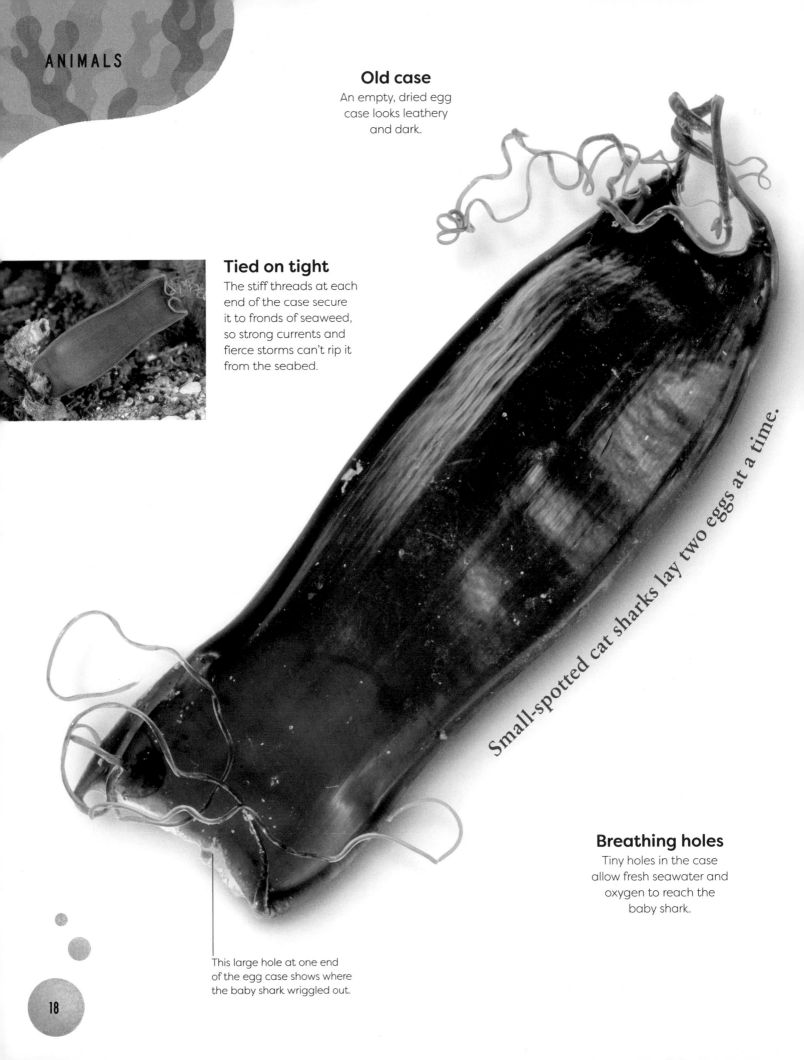

Old case
An empty, dried egg case looks leathery and dark.

Tied on tight
The stiff threads at each end of the case secure it to fronds of seaweed, so strong currents and fierce storms can't rip it from the seabed.

Small-spotted cat sharks lay two eggs at a time.

Breathing holes
Tiny holes in the case allow fresh seawater and oxygen to reach the baby shark.

This large hole at one end of the egg case shows where the baby shark wriggled out.

Mermaid's purse

Some sharks, skates, and rays lay mysterious egg cases, which wind up on beaches.

Not so long ago, people thought the sea was full of monsters and other mythical creatures. So it is hardly surprising that this curious object was given some pretty odd names, including mermaid's purse and witch's purse. We now know it is really an egg case, produced by some sharks and by related fish called skates and rays. The cases have a surface like tough leather and may be yellow, brown, or black, with horns or curly threads at each corner. They are also slightly see-through, which makes it possible to see the babies wriggling inside.

Once the sharks have hatched, the empty cases sometimes wash ashore, often after rough seas. Some might even still be attached to the seaweed they were secured to by the mother shark. With an opening at one end, an old egg case would have made the perfect purse for a mermaid. The seashore air usually shrivels the cases and turns them darker, but if they are washed back into the sea, the water returns them to their original color, texture, and shape!

Small-spotted cat shark
(Scyliorhinus canicula)
This little shark grows no bigger than 3 ft (1 m) long. It lives in the coastal waters of the northeastern Atlantic Ocean.

Developing shark

Hatching shark

Growing a shark
A female cat shark lays her eggs among seaweed. Each case contains a yolk that feeds the growing baby, or embryo. After seven to 10 months of development, the young shark, also called a pup, bites its way out of the case.

Egg

19

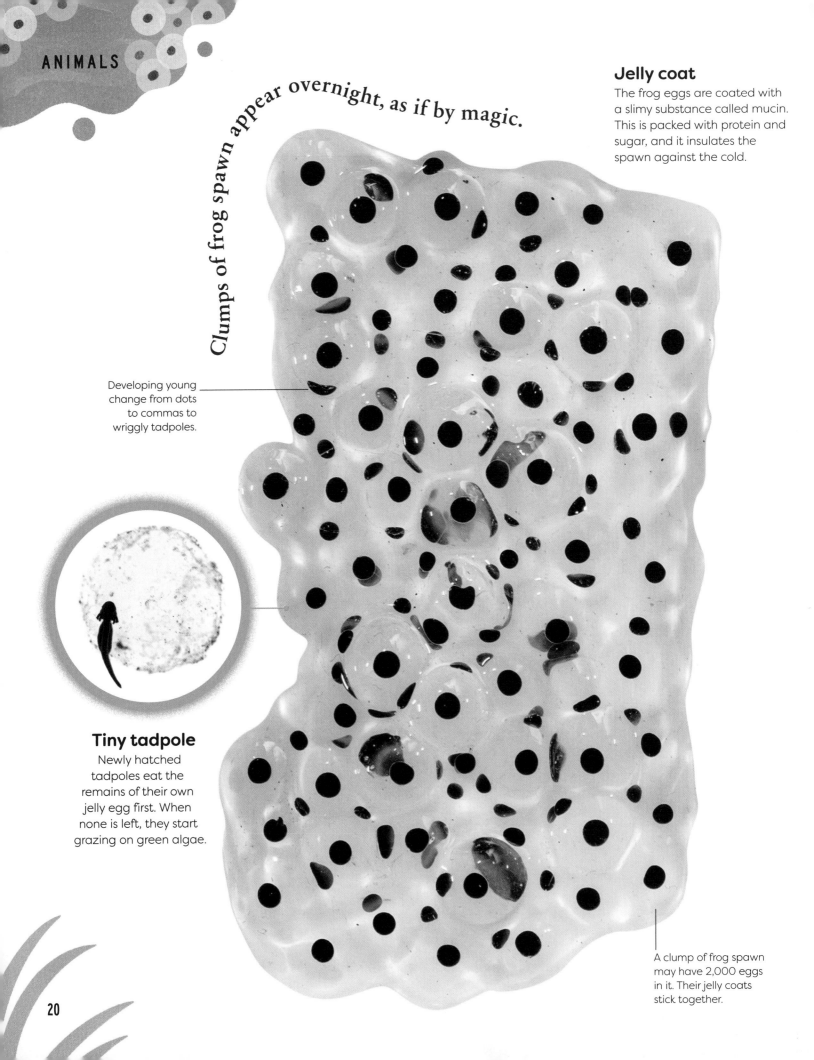

Clumps of frog spawn appear overnight, as if by magic.

Jelly coat
The frog eggs are coated with a slimy substance called mucin. This is packed with protein and sugar, and it insulates the spawn against the cold.

Developing young change from dots to commas to wriggly tadpoles.

Tiny tadpole
Newly hatched tadpoles eat the remains of their own jelly egg first. When none is left, they start grazing on green algae.

A clump of frog spawn may have 2,000 eggs in it. Their jelly coats stick together.

Frog spawn

Jellylike frog spawn is a sign that spring is just around the corner.

Every species of frog on Earth lays eggs. To prevent them from drying out as they develop, the eggs usually have to be left in clean freshwater, most often a pond, but even a puddle will do. As winter loses its grip on northern Europe, and days get longer again, the increase in daylight tells common frogs to march to their breeding ponds. They breed on mild, rainy nights between February and April. The next morning, always in the sunniest part of the pond, you will find slimy clumps of eggs, known as frog spawn. Often several female frogs lay their spawn together, and it merges to form wobbly mounds. After a day or two, the spawn swells up, as it takes on water. Why, though, do common frogs lay so many eggs? The answer is that a lot of the spawn and young frogs, called tadpoles, are eaten by predators, such as ducks, water beetle larvae, and otters. A female needs to produce as many young as possible to be sure that some will survive to adulthood.

Common frog
(*Rana temporaria*)

Found throughout northern Europe, these frogs cope well with cool conditions. In Scandinavia, they live as far north as the Arctic.

Older tadpole

Froglet

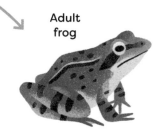

Adult frog

Young tadpole

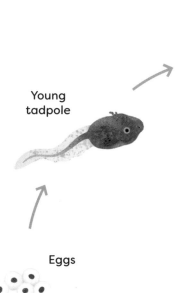

Eggs

Total transformation

Frog spawn is just the start of a frog's life. Baby tadpoles hatch from the eggs and breathe using frilly external gills. At 8–12 weeks, their legs appear. After 12 weeks, the tail is lost, and by 16 weeks, the froglets are fully formed and can now breathe air.

Feather

Only birds have feathers. They are light but strong and come in many brilliant colors.

Among the fall leaves is a dazzling blue feather. Once it formed part of a jay's wing, until the bird molted it. The feather weighs next to nothing and is soft and delicate. Yet it is also tough and waterproof. This winning combination is why feathers are unbelievably useful to birds. In all, a jay has around 5,000 of them, but a tiny hummingbird might possess just 1,000, and a swan could have 25,000.

Feathers come in many types, every one of which has a job to do. Masses of small feathers cover a bird's body to create a smooth surface. Underneath these, close to the skin, is a snug layer of soft, fluffy feathers, called down, which trap heat and keep the bird warm. Large wing feathers create wings that allow the bird to lift itself into the air, and long tail feathers help it steer and keep its balance. All feathers are made of the protein keratin, which also makes up our hair and fingernails. This is sturdy enough to survive in fossils, which is how we know that many dinosaurs were feathery, too, and that—amazingly—birds are dinosaurs!

Eurasian jay
(Garrulus glandarius)
Jays are colorful woodland crows that are mainly found in Asia and Europe. When excited or alarmed, they raise the feathers on the top of their heads.

Strong structure
A feather's main stem, called a shaft, has many thin branches, called barbs, which line up on each side like the teeth of a comb. In turn, the barbs have even thinner branches, called barbules. These are held tightly together with tiny hooks.

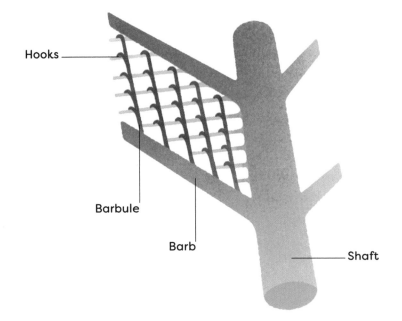

Hooks

Barbule

Barb

Shaft

Feathers for flight

Birds can spread their wing feathers, which creates a large surface to push against the air and helps them fly.

Birds run their beak through their feathers to rehook separated barbules.

The visible parts of the feather appear colorful.

Blue... or brown?

This wing feather is actually brown and black! The brown areas appear blue because of how they scatter sunlight.

The hidden parts of the feather are white.

Near the body of the bird, the feather is fluffy to help trap precious heat.

The shaft is hollow at the base, but the rest of it is solid.

23

Feathers

Feathers are one of the key features of birds, and they have an impact on every aspect of a bird's life. Each feather may be stiff or soft, flat or curved, narrow or wide, plain or patterned, smaller than a human fingernail or more than 5 ft (1.5 m) long.

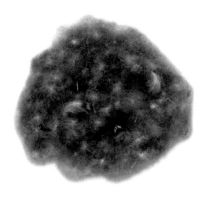

American flamingo
The stunning rosy color of this flamingo wing feather comes from pigments in the bird's main food source, shrimp. If the flamingo stops eating shrimp, the pink soon fades to white.

Common eider
This clump of supersoft down feathers is from a female eider duck. She plucks them to line her nest. People collect the warm feathers to fill comforters and pillows.

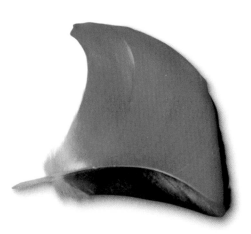

Mandarin duck
The mandarin duck is from eastern Asia. Males have a pair of what look like bright orange sails on their backs, each of which is a large, stiff wing feather.

Ostrich
Ostrich wing and body feathers are so fluffy they are made into feather dusters. Because the giant birds are too heavy to take off, they don't need strong feathers for flight.

Great argus
The markings on this feather give superb camouflage among the leafy shadows of the rain forest floor, where this species of pheasant spends most of its time.

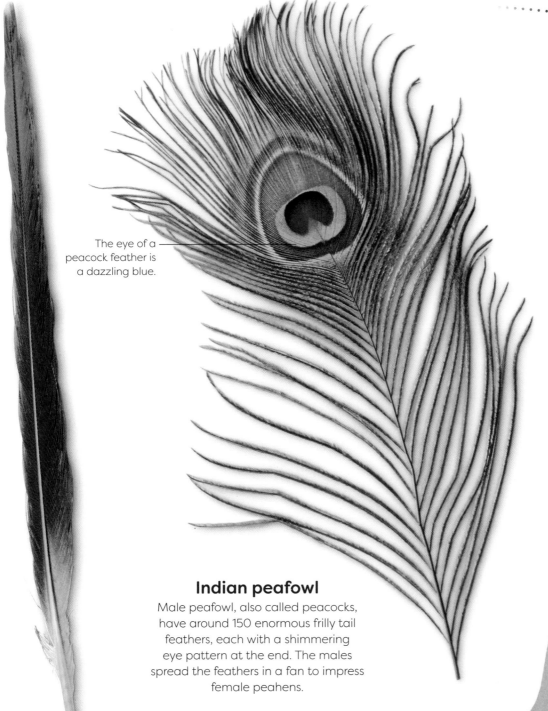

The eye of a peacock feather is a dazzling blue.

Tawny owl

An owl's wing feathers have frayed edges that muffle the sound of air moving past. This gives the owl silent flight, so it can swoop down on prey completely by surprise.

Indian peafowl

Male peafowl, also called peacocks, have around 150 enormous frilly tail feathers, each with a shimmering eye pattern at the end. The males spread the feathers in a fan to impress female peahens.

Filoplume

Semiplume

Down

Ring-necked parakeet

This parakeet has a pointed tail made up of 12 feathers. Amazingly, the central tail feathers are up to 8 in (20 cm) long—around half the total length of the bird!

Feather shapes

Every bird has feathers of several types, all of which have different jobs to do. Wing and tail feathers are strong and firm, whereas many body feathers are fluffy at the bottom for maximum warmth. Down is warmest of all. Some feathers are just for showing off.

Wing feather

Tail feather

Dragonfly wings

Dragonflies are the fastest and most agile insects—and it is all thanks to their wings.

When you watch a dragonfly zoom around over a pond, remember this: its gigantic, bird-sized relatives were doing the same thing 300 million years ago. These supersized relations were among the very first creatures to take to the skies, long before most other insects. Today, dragonflies have inspired engineers who are trying to create new types of tiny drones. Like the insects, these have four wings that move independently. This unique ability is what gives dragonflies their amazing agility. Dragonflies have sensational acceleration, but they can also come to a dramatic stop in midair. They can hover and do sudden turns, vertical ascents, and loop the loops. They can even fly backward.

As a result of their aerial acrobatic skills, dragonflies are fearsome predators, able to chase down all kinds of insect prey—even smaller dragonflies! A dragonfly's wings are powered by massive muscles housed in the middle part of its body. These are so big that on a cool day the insect may need to warm them up by basking in the sun or whirring its wings before takeoff.

Common darter
(*Sympetrum striolatum*)
In much of Europe, these are one of the most common dragonflies. Males have orange-red bodies, whereas females are yellow-brown.

Fast flyer
Dragonflies usually beat their two pairs of wings alternately. Their front wings push down, while their back wings move up, then they swap positions. If you watch a dragonfly head on, the overall effect is like a whirring "X" shape.

Back wing

Front wing

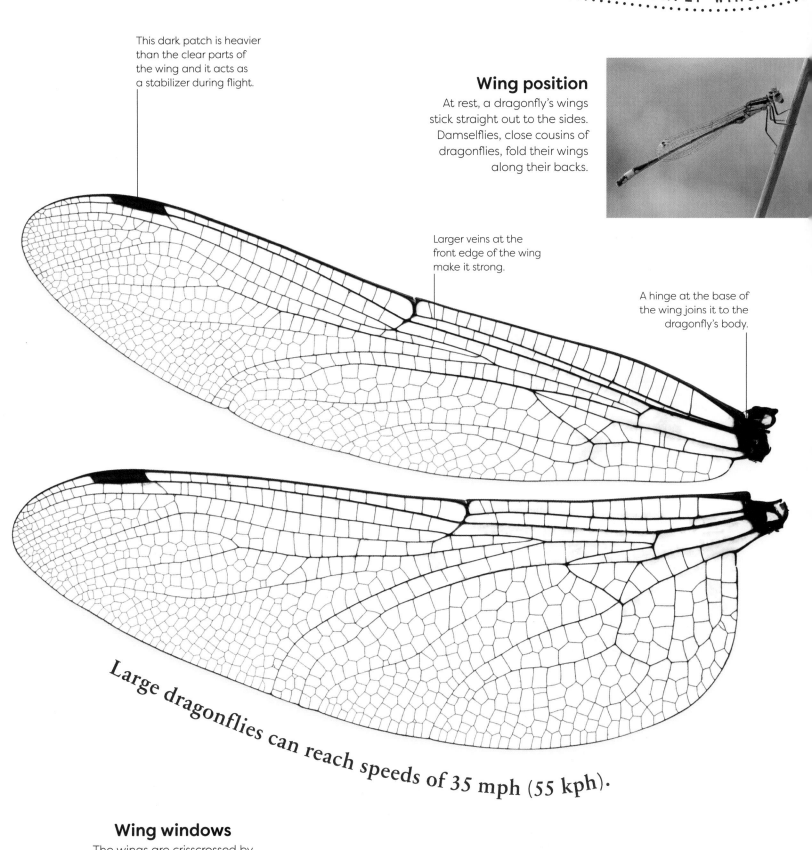

This dark patch is heavier than the clear parts of the wing and it acts as a stabilizer during flight.

Wing position

At rest, a dragonfly's wings stick straight out to the sides. Damselflies, close cousins of dragonflies, fold their wings along their backs.

Larger veins at the front edge of the wing make it strong.

A hinge at the base of the wing joins it to the dragonfly's body.

Large dragonflies can reach speeds of 35 mph (55 kph).

Wing windows

The wings are crisscrossed by a network of veins that act as strengthening rods. The areas between them, called cells, are as clear as glass.

27

A short stalk attaches the scale to the wing.

Glittering wing

Some butterfly wings, such as those of blue morpho butterflies, seem to glitter. This effect, called iridescence, is caused by tiny grooves in the scales.

The scale is made of chitin, which is also found in insect skeletons.

Every scale is a jewel-like flake of color.

Toothed edge

Some scales are short, with a straight edge. The longest scales end in several points and look like a duck's webbed foot.

Butterfly scale

A butterfly's wing is a living collage created from row upon row of tiny scales.

The wing of a butterfly is an extraordinary thing. It is strong yet flexible, and inside it there are sensors that detect light and temperature. There is even a little "wing heart" that pumps butterfly blood to every corner of it. The surface of the wing is equally amazing. It is built from thousands of scales, which are too small for us to see easily. Each one is no more than 0.004 in (0.1 mm) long—this is roughly the thickness of a human hair. The scales can be many different colors, and, like the pixels on a screen, together they produce complex patterns.

The male eastern tiger swallowtail butterfly has a bright and bold wing pattern that helps it attract a mate. However, some butterflies use camouflage to blend in with bark or leaves. There is an extra advantage to scaly wings. If a butterfly is attacked by a bird or becomes stuck in a spider's web, it can shed scales to escape. The butterfly is left with bare patches, because the scales don't grow back, but at least it has made its getaway.

Eastern tiger swallowtail
(Papilio glaucus)
This common butterfly flits through flowery meadows and gardens in the eastern half of North America.

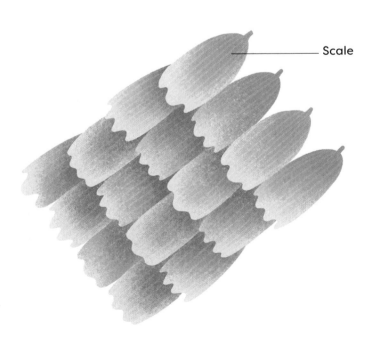

Scale

Overlapping scales
Butterfly scales are thin and flat. They fit together in neat rows across the wing. Each row overlaps the next one, just like the tiles on a roof. At the base of each scale is a short stalk that secures it to the wing.

The shedding process

The snake starts by rubbing its head against a rough surface. When the skin on its head splits, the snake wriggles to make the tear larger, then slides out. It emerges in its fresh skin, which is bright and shiny.

Pigment pattern

The beautiful colors in snakeskin are produced by several pigments, one of which is melanin, also found in human skin.

Shed skin

Old skin

New skin

You can still see hints of the original pattern on the shed skin.

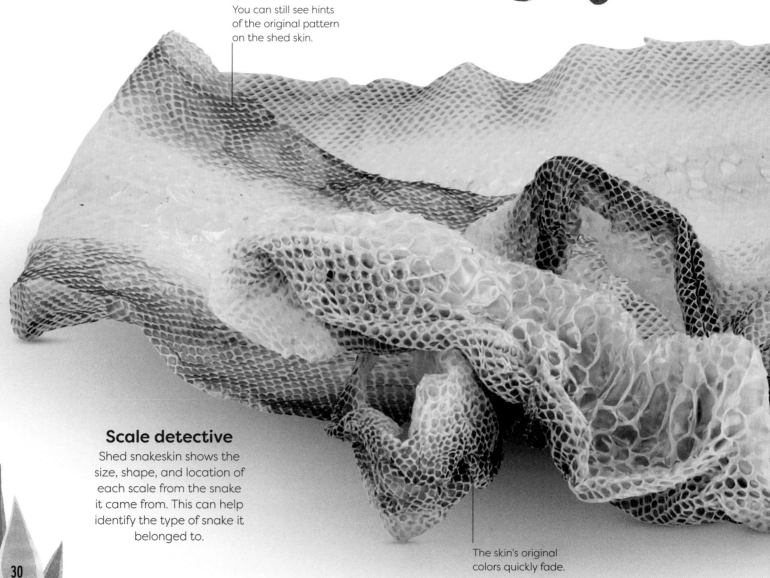

Scale detective

Shed snakeskin shows the size, shape, and location of each scale from the snake it came from. This can help identify the type of snake it belonged to.

The skin's original colors quickly fade.

Shed snakeskin

Between one and four times a year, snakes squeeze out of their skin to reveal a new one underneath.

You may not realize it, but humans constantly shed their skin. On average, we lose nearly a million skin cells a day! These are quickly replaced, as our skin keeps on regenerating. However, many animals, such as snakes and lizards, change all their skin at once. Over time, a snake's skin gets damaged and worn. It needs replacing, in the way we replace worn-out clothes. The skin is stretchy enough to allow some growth, but in fast-growing young snakes skin needs to be replaced more often. Another benefit to the snake is that any parasites living on it are removed with the old skin.

A perfect shed snakeskin is a ghostly outline of the whole snake. You can even see where its eyes were. This is because snakes have a single clear scale over each eye, and these special scales peel away with the rest of the skin. There is no sign of the snake's ears though, because these are hidden inside its heads. It is a myth that the skin on a living snake is slimy. In fact, snakes feel smooth and dry, as does their shed snakeskin.

The scale imprints are neatly organized in long rows.

Royal python
(Python regius)
The royal python lives in western and central Africa. It is also called a ball python, because this snake rolls into a ball when attacked.

31

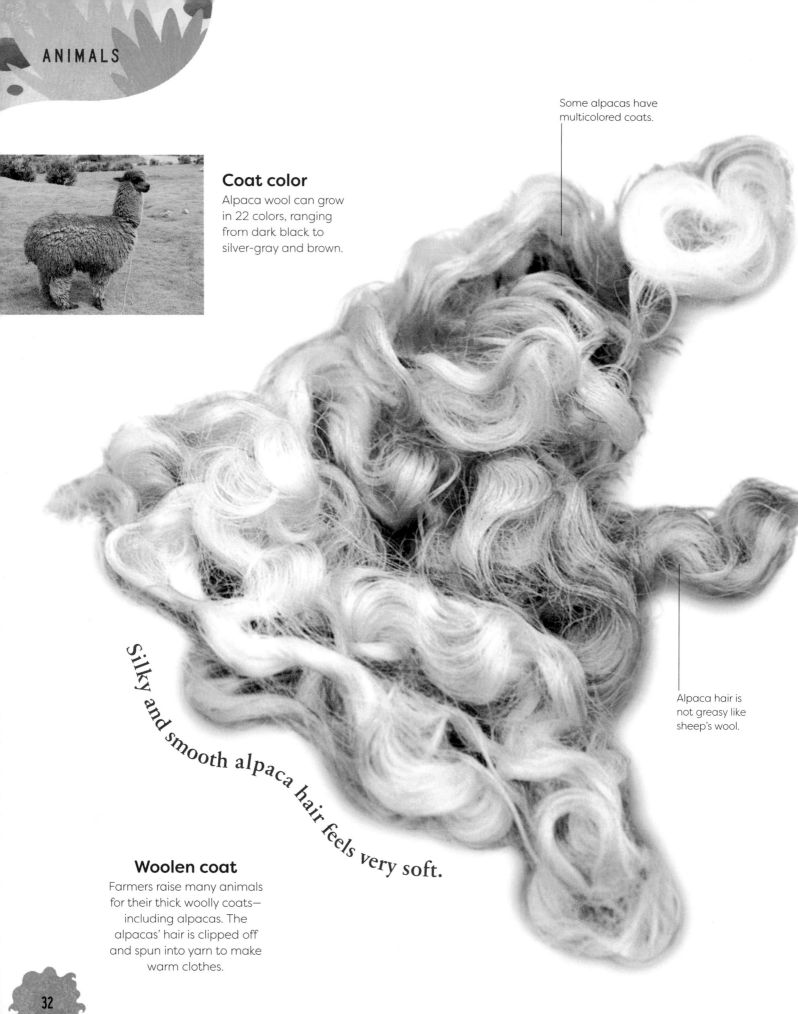

Coat color
Alpaca wool can grow in 22 colors, ranging from dark black to silver-gray and brown.

Some alpacas have multicolored coats.

Alpaca hair is not greasy like sheep's wool.

Silky and smooth alpaca hair feels very soft.

Woolen coat
Farmers raise many animals for their thick woolly coats—including alpacas. The alpacas' hair is clipped off and spun into yarn to make warm clothes.

Alpaca wool

Tufts of soft, curly hair are just what an alpaca needs to stay warm and cozy.

Wool is the name for very thick fur made from many curly hairs. In addition to alpacas, several other kinds of animals have lovely warm woolly coats, including sheep, goats, and yaks. All of these animals are part of a much bigger group—mammals. Hair is one of the key features of mammals. Even smooth-bodied sea mammals such as whales and dolphins have a few thick bristly hairs deep inside their nostrils.

Each hair grows from a root in the skin. It takes about a month for human hairs to grow by about half an inch (1 cm). The hair itself is not alive. Instead, it is made from a flexible and waterproof protein called keratin. The main job of hair is to keep the body warm and dry, but it can do other things, too. Hedgehogs and porcupines have very thick, pointed hairs that make sharp spikes for defense. A cat's whiskers are touch-sensing hairs that work as feelers. Meanwhile, your hairy eyelashes catch any dust and grit so it doesn't get in your eyes.

Alpaca
(Vicugna pacos)
The alpaca is a relative of the camel—but without a hump. It lives in the cold and windy Andes mountains of South America.

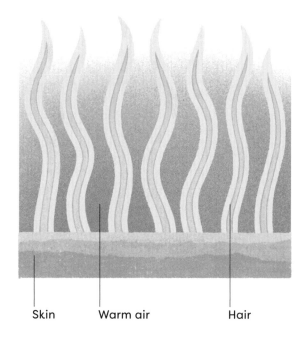

Skin Warm air Hair

Keeping cozy
Mammals like to be toasty and keep their bodies warmer than the surrounding air. A coat of hair helps by trapping a layer of warm air close to the skin. In many animals the coat thickens at colder times of the year.

33

Fish scale

A scaly body keeps fish safe and healthy and helps them swim more efficiently.

Why don't fish have an all-in-one body covering similar to the wetsuits humans wear? It is an interesting question, but scales provide many advantages. For a start, they are thin, so they don't weigh much. Scales are also tough, offering the fish protection. They can move slightly, too, which makes the fish more flexible and allows it to change its position in the water quickly. Many scales have grooves or ridges that improve the flow of water across them, too. All this means that a scaly fish can slip through water more easily than if its body had a single outer layer.

Yet another benefit of scales is that they can be replaced. If a fish is attacked, it can afford to shed individual scales. They flake off, leaving the predator in a glittering cloud while the fish escapes. Many fish also coat their scales in slime to deter parasites. In some fish, this slimy coating contains deadly toxins to put off predators. The slime of one pufferfish may be strong enough to kill several humans.

Ballan wrasse
(Labrus bergylta)
These colorful fish live mainly on rocky shores in Europe, from southern Scandinavia to France. Young wrasse are greenish, which helps them hide from predators.

Streamlined skin
Most fish scales overlap slightly, creating a smooth surface. However, they are only attached along the front edge. This enables the fish to raise them if needed, allowing it to move more easily.

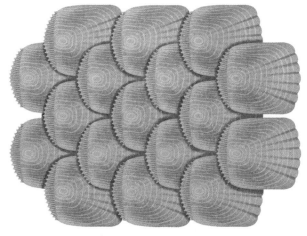

Front of fish ⟶

Shark scales

Shark scales, such as those of the nursehound shark, have a different structure than those of other fish. They are more like tiny teeth with sharp points.

A fan of ridges and grooves is hidden under other scales.

If scales are lost, they regrow in a few weeks.

Adult ballan wrasse are covered in spots. This scale has one large dot on it.

Patterns with purpose

Many fish, including wrasse, have pretty patterns on their scales, which can make them stand out or help them hide. Only the visible part of the scale is colorful.

Each scale is thin and flat, but it is not fixed down to the skin underneath.

An expert in seashells is called a conchologist.

The ridges make the thin shell very strong.

Thin lines in the shell show how it has grown over time.

The upper shell is much flatter than the curved one underneath.

The two shells connect to each other at this hinge.

Swimming scallop
The scallop moves by clapping its shells together over and over. That forces little jets of water out of holes in the hinge, and the scallop whizzes through the water.

Smooth sides
Scallop shells are rough on the outside, but smooth inside. The shiny interior prevents damage to the scallop's soft body.

Scallop shell

Shaped like a little fan, a scallop shell is a place to live, a suit of armor, plus a way of getting around.

Hard and rough on the outside, but soft and delicate inside, the scallop is a beautiful example of a bivalve mollusk. Mollusks are a huge group of animals with soft, squishy bodies that includes snails, octopuses, and bivalves. Snails are famous for living inside one shell. Octopuses have no shell at all, while bivalves, such as scallops, oysters, and clams, have a pair of shells connected by a hinge. The two shells are also called valves. All mollusk shells are made from chalky white calcium carbonate, but many are brightly colored and patterned. As the scallop grows, it adds more layers to the outer edge of its shells, so its body is always protected.

Many mollusks are sea animals. Scallops sit on the sandy seabed. Like most bivalves, they do not hunt. When they are hungry, all they have to do is open their shells and filter out tiny scraps of food from the water. If the tide goes out, the scallop will clamp its valves tightly shut so it traps water inside to keep it moist and cool until the sea covers it again.

Red scallop
(Pecten fumatus)
This scallop lives near Australia. The tentacles poking out from the shell check for food in the water.

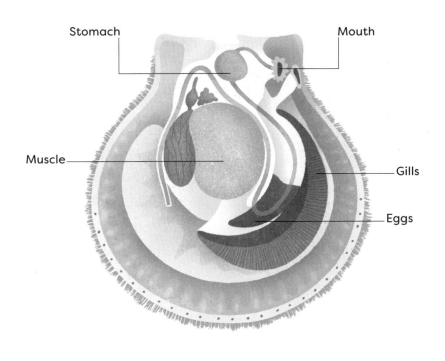

Stomach · Mouth · Muscle · Gills · Eggs

Inside a scallop

The central part of a scallop's soft body is a strong muscle that pulls the two shells closed. The scallop's other body parts loop around it, with the mouth and stomach near the hinge. Large gills take oxygen from the water.

37

Shells

Shells are structures that support and protect the animal inside. Many invertebrates produce them, especially mollusks such as gastropods, bivalves, and cephalopods. Empty shells have been used all over the world as jewelry and money.

Purple dye murex

These Mediterranean sea snails have a shell with a long, spiked "tail." In ancient times, the shells were boiled to make a fabulous purple dye used for clothes worn by rulers and judges.

Chambered nautilus

The big, beautiful shells of these unusual cephalopods have a pearly shine. Inside are spiraling chambers that fill with water or gas to help the animal rise or sink, much like a submarine.

Asian green mussel

Green mussels are found along rocky shores in clusters known as mussel beds. When submerged, they open to filter food from the water. Their empty shells are perfectly smooth and white inside.

Garden snail

The shells of these common snails keep growing: the larger the shell, the older the snail. Nearly all their shells spiral to the right, but in rare instances they spiral to the left.

Red-footed conch

Many sea snails, such as conches, have handsome spiral patterns on their shells. Conches are fierce predators of worms and can also drill into and attack other snails.

Greater argonaut

The argonaut is a type of octopus, and this amazing object is the female's nursery. It is not a true shell but a frilly, paper-thin case used to keep her eggs safe.

Growth rings show how the shell has grown throughout the animal's life.

Grooved razor shell

Razor shells, also called razor clams, are bivalves. They have a hinge along one long side and burrow in seashore sand. They often wash up empty on beaches after storms.

Venus comb

Some sea snails in the murex family have spectacular spines. These protect the snails, making them an impossible mouthful for predators, and stop them from sinking into the muddy seabed.

Venus comb shells can have dozens of sharp spines.

Shell types

There are three main groups of mollusks with shells. Bivalves, such as mussels and clams, have two-part shells joined by a hinge. Gastropods, such as snails, have coiled or twisted shells. Cephalopods, such as squid, octopuses, and nautiluses, can have outer shells or hidden internal shells.

Bivalve

Gastropod

Cephalopod

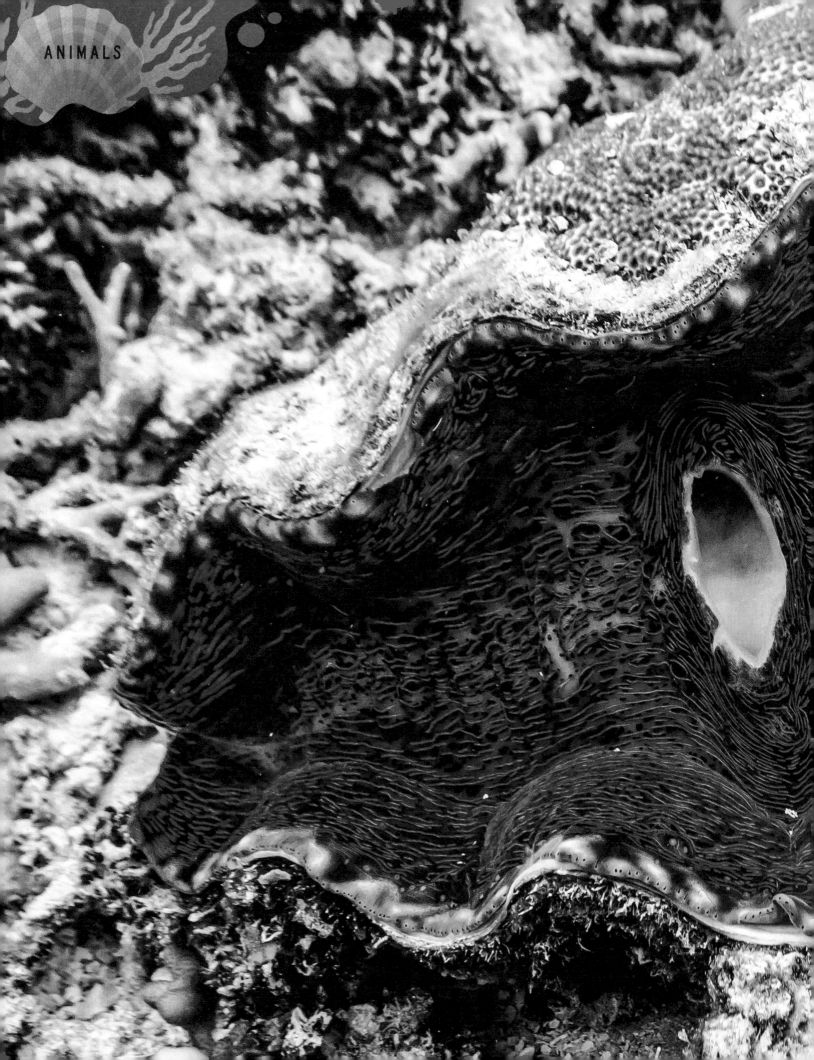

Giant shell

The world's largest shell belongs to the giant clam, which can grow as wide as a double bed, weigh more than 440 lb (200 kg), and live longer than a century. Eventually, the shell becomes too big to close completely. The clam obtains most of its food from the algae that live inside its colorful body.

Polyp cups
The surface of the coral skeleton is covered in hundreds of cuplike dents—one for each polyp to live in.

Thinner branches spread from a central trunk, just like a tree.

Coral skeletons can look like fans, mushrooms, or antlers.

Dead, but red
Even though it is dead, this coral skeleton has kept its red color, which is produced by the same pigments as those in fall leaves and carrots.

When a new coral colony begins, it attaches itself to the seafloor.

Coral skeleton

Corals are magicians that conjure skeletons for themselves from the seawater they live in.

Red coral looks like a fiery bush with bright branches, but some things are not what they seem. Corals are animals, not plants. The first person to realize this was a Persian scientist named Al-Biruni, who lived a thousand years ago. He noticed that corals responded if something touched them. What Al-Biruni didn't know was that every coral is many tiny animals joined permanently together. Each one is called a polyp, and it has a simple, soft body.

By living together in a colony, polyps gain strength in numbers and can build a large, hard skeleton that protects them all. The polyps take the mineral calcium carbonate from the water and use it to form a stony structure. As new polyps bud off from old polyps, they too get to work, and the structure slowly grows. When many coral colonies live in the same place, they can create a coral reef—some of which are big enough to be visible from space! If a coral dies, the skeleton is all that remains.

Red coral
(Corallium rubrum)
This bright coral lives in the waters of the Mediterranean Sea, often on rocks or in caves.

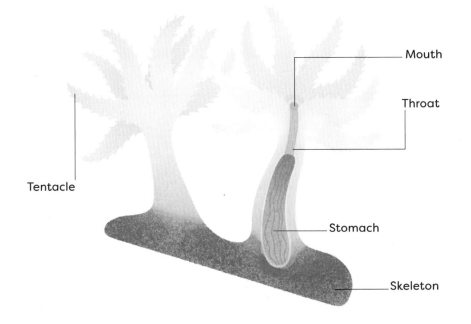

Mouth

Throat

Tentacle

Stomach

Skeleton

Coral polyp

A polyp is just a few millimeters long and is little more than a tube with a mouth and stomach. To feed, it pushes out eight tentacles armed with stingers, which paralyze prey. The mouth also acts as a bottom!

Cicada case

The empty case of a cicada nymph is a perfect cast of the creature that once lived inside.

Most insects undergo dramatic transformations during their lifetimes. Many have two life stages: larva and adult, which are spent in different habitats, eating different foods. The larva and adult often look so different that it can be difficult to believe they are the same species! Butterflies make this change during a single spectacular transformation, which happens inside a chrysalis. Moths, ants, bees, flies, and beetles do something similar. However, most other insects go through several more gradual changes.

This is what the periodical cicada does. It spends years buried in the earth as a white, wingless larva called a nymph. While underground, the nymph changes its skin five times, and each time it emerges with a slightly different body shape. When the nymph is ready, it digs itself out of the ground, climbs a tree, and sheds its skin for the sixth and final time. It bursts out of its old nymph skin as a fully-grown adult. Large groups of nymphs often appear above ground at the same time. The empty case each leaves behind is dry and crispy, and is a perfect cast of its former body.

Periodical cicada
(Magicicada septendecim)
The nymphs of this North American cicada eat tree roots underground for 17 years, then emerge in the spring to turn into adults.

The case shows short stubs instead of full-size wings.

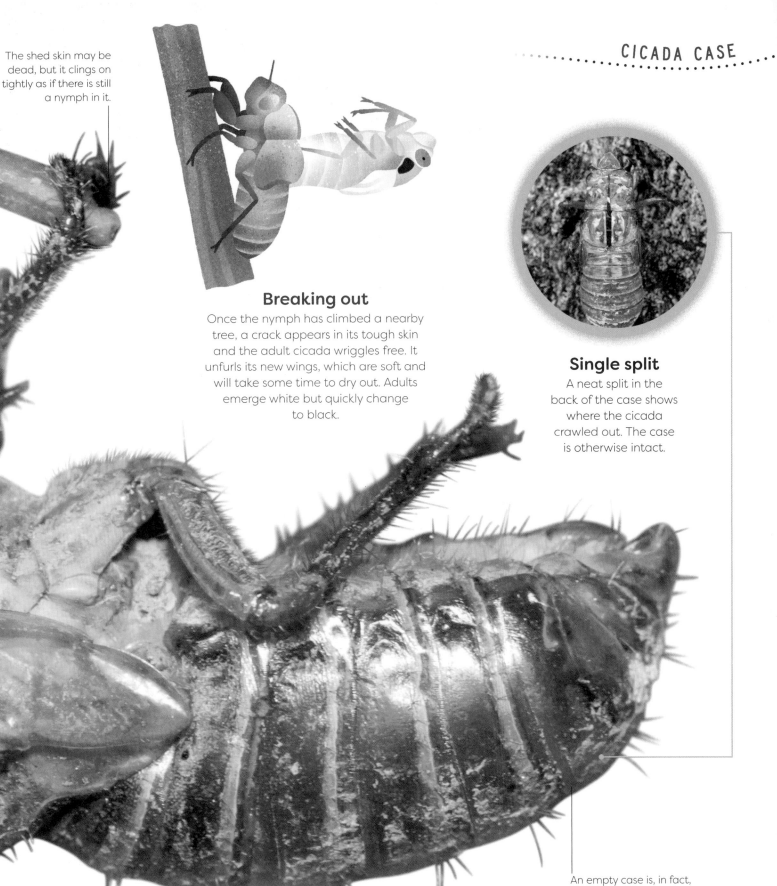

The shed skin may be dead, but it clings on tightly as if there is still a nymph in it.

Breaking out

Once the nymph has climbed a nearby tree, a crack appears in its tough skin and the adult cicada wriggles free. It unfurls its new wings, which are soft and will take some time to dry out. Adults emerge white but quickly change to black.

Single split

A neat split in the back of the case shows where the cicada crawled out. The case is otherwise intact.

An empty case is, in fact, the shed outer skeleton that covered the whole nymph—including the hairs on its body.

Trillions of periodical cicadas emerge at the same time.

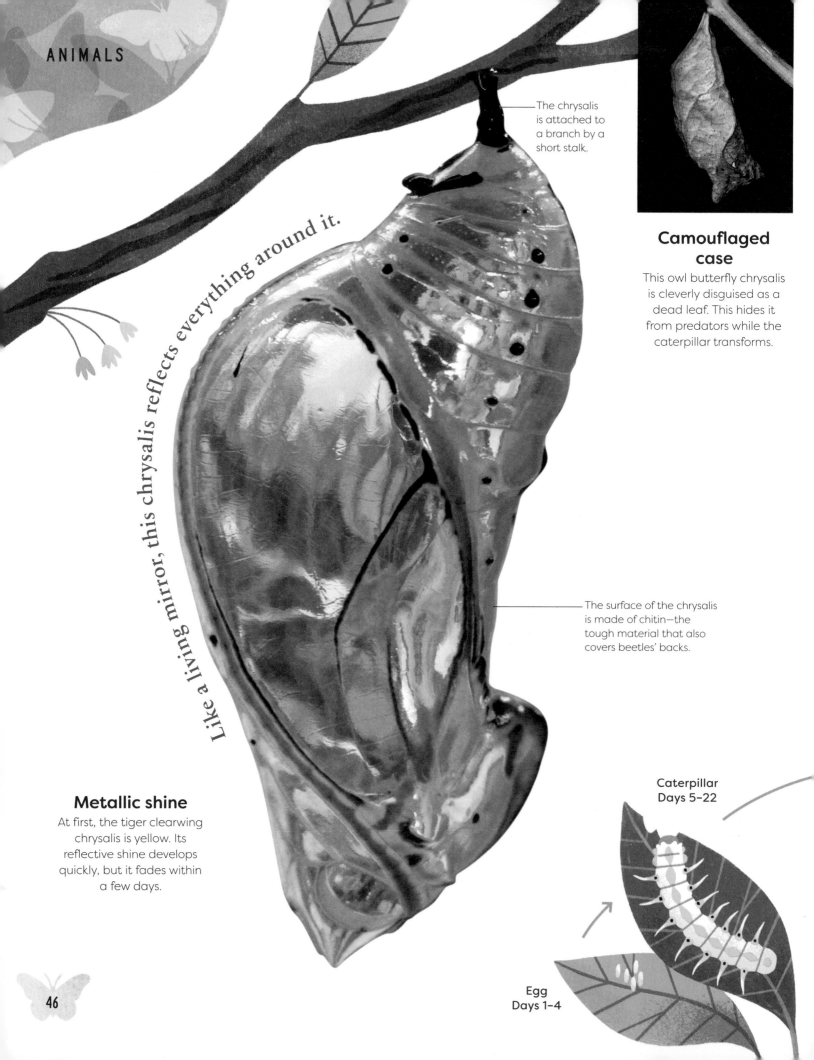

The chrysalis is attached to a branch by a short stalk.

Camouflaged case

This owl butterfly chrysalis is cleverly disguised as a dead leaf. This hides it from predators while the caterpillar transforms.

Like a living mirror, this chrysalis reflects everything around it.

The surface of the chrysalis is made of chitin—the tough material that also covers beetles' backs.

Metallic shine

At first, the tiger clearwing chrysalis is yellow. Its reflective shine develops quickly, but it fades within a few days.

Caterpillar
Days 5–22

Egg
Days 1–4

Chrysalis

A fat caterpillar forms this protective pod around itself while it transforms into a spectacular fluttering butterfly.

On a rain forest trail something glitters among the lush green leaves. About as long as a human thumbnail, it gleams like gold. Suddenly, it twitches. It is very much alive. The shiny chrysalis, or pupa, has been created by a caterpillar to protect its soft body while it changes into a tiger clearwing butterfly. Every butterfly on Earth develops this way. From the outside, a chrysalis seems to be asleep, but under its skin, the caterpillar has turned into a soup of cells and is busy rebuilding itself as a butterfly. During this full-body makeover, called metamorphosis, the chrysalis can still feel and breathe. Some chrysalises can even twitter or squeak! Maybe this frightens away hungry birds.

Many chrysalises have another defense, too: they are camouflaged as dead leaves, sticks, or bird poop. Perhaps being shiny is also camouflage—the metallic tiger clearwing chrysalis may reflect its surroundings and blend into the background, making it invisible to its predators. No one knows.

Orange-spotted tiger clearwing
(*Mechanitis polymnia*)
This butterfly lives in tropical rain forests from Mexico to Brazil. Adult clearwings look very different from their caterpillars.

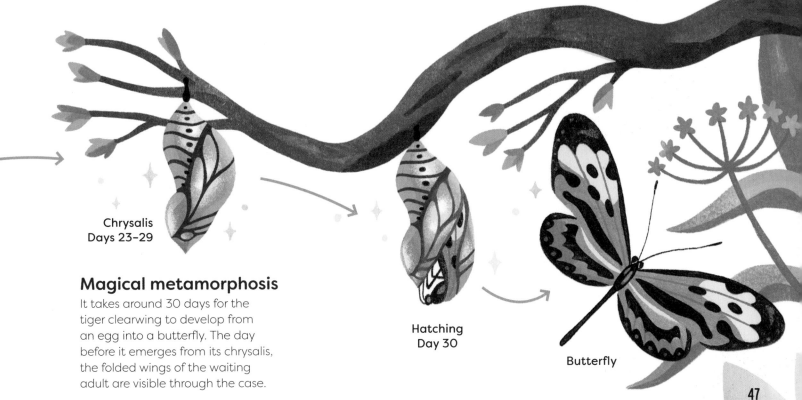

Chrysalis
Days 23–29

Magical metamorphosis
It takes around 30 days for the tiger clearwing to develop from an egg into a butterfly. The day before it emerges from its chrysalis, the folded wings of the waiting adult are visible through the case.

Hatching
Day 30

Butterfly

47

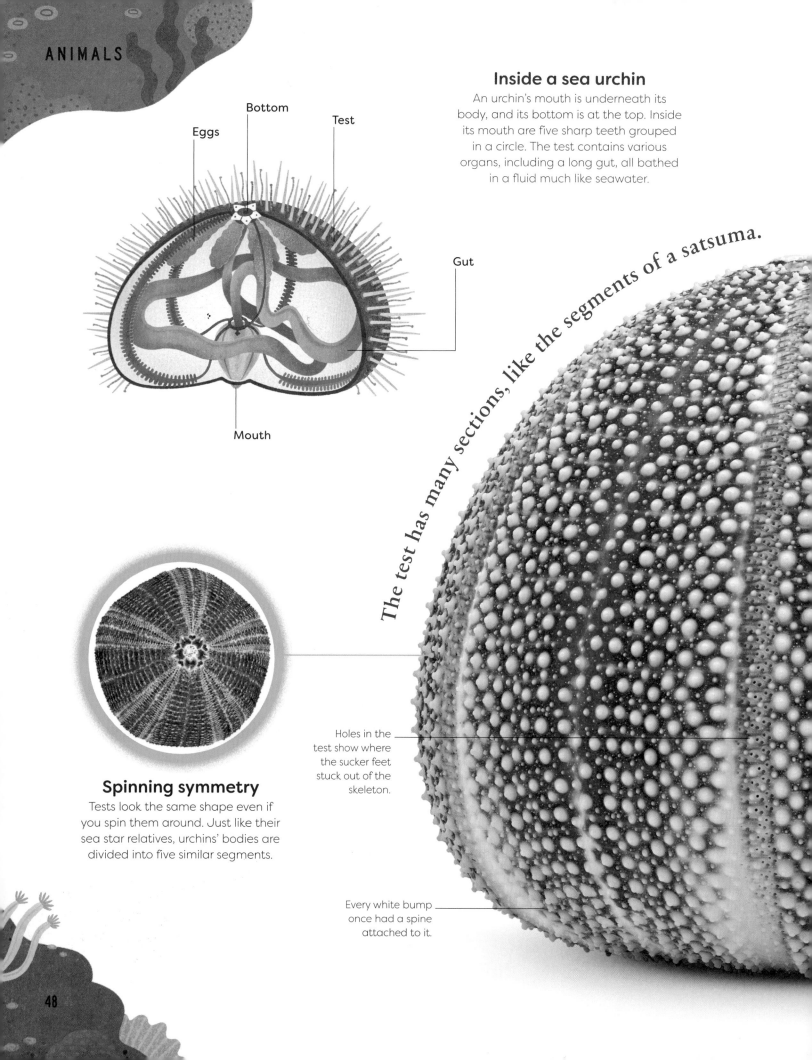

Eggs

Bottom

Test

Inside a sea urchin

An urchin's mouth is underneath its body, and its bottom is at the top. Inside its mouth are five sharp teeth grouped in a circle. The test contains various organs, including a long gut, all bathed in a fluid much like seawater.

Gut

The test has many sections, like the segments of a satsuma.

Mouth

Spinning symmetry

Tests look the same shape even if you spin them around. Just like their sea star relatives, urchins' bodies are divided into five similar segments.

Holes in the test show where the sucker feet stuck out of the skeleton.

Every white bump once had a spine attached to it.

Sea urchin test

When a sea urchin dies, its spines fall off and its insides rot, leaving just its delicate skeleton behind.

Sea urchins have been on Earth for around 540 million years. Their shell-like skeletons, called tests, can wash up on the seashore like fragile marine treasure. Sometimes an empty test rattles because the urchin's hard teeth and jaws are too large to fall out of the hole at the bottom, where the urchin's mouth once was. When it is alive, an urchin's hard test provides protection and support for the organs inside it. Often the tests seen on beaches have faded, but living ones can be bright pink, purple, blue, black, or green.

Urchins look a little like underwater hedgehogs. Their bodies are covered in long, sharp spines that can move in different directions to put off predators. Some species have venomous pinchers, too. Between the spines, there are 10 rows of delicate sucker feet that the urchin uses to creep around, even upside down. The skin of the feet is so thin that oxygen can pass through it, and they have sensors to detect light. This means sea urchins breathe and see with their feet!

Common sea urchin
(*Echinus esculentus*)
Algae and seaweed are the favorite food of these urchins. They graze in herds off the coast of northwest Europe, leaving bare patches on the seabed.

49

Invertebrate skeletons

Around 97 percent of all animals are invertebrates. They all lack a backbone, or spine. In fact, they don't have a single bone in their bodies. Many rely on an external skeleton—an exoskeleton—for support and protection. A few have internal skeletons.

European common squid

Squid are mollusks, like snails. However, their shells have become flat, narrow structures that grow inside their bodies like a skeleton. These look like old writing quills so are also known as pens.

Eccentric sand dollar

The disklike skeleton of this sea urchin resembles an old dollar coin. The flowery pattern is created by many tiny holes, through which the sand dollar extended its breathing organs.

Venus flower basket

This deep-sea animal is a kind of sponge with a tubelike skeleton made from delicate glassy struts. Holes in the skeleton allow the sponge to suck in water and filter food from it.

Fiddler crab

Crabs are built like tanks, with an armored exoskeleton that covers the entire body, including their legs and claws. Fiddler crabs have one enormous claw, which is used for showing off.

Jewel beetle

The toughest parts of a beetle's exoskeleton are its two solid wing cases, which protect its wings. Jewel beetles have brightly colored wing cases that shimmer and shine.

Common cuttlefish

Cuttlefish have a flat, skeleton-like internal structure called a cuttlefish bone—although it is not made of bone. These structures often wash up on beaches like tiny white surfboards.

Arthropod

Echinoderm

Cephalopod

Inside or outside?

Arthropods, such as insects and crabs, have a hard case outside their bodies: an exoskeleton. Echinoderms, such as sea urchins, have a skeleton inside. The skeleton-like structures in cephalopods, such as cuttlefish, are actually internal shells.

A long tail flips the animal upright if it gets overturned.

Atlantic horseshoe crab

These ancient marine creatures have shieldlike exoskeletons and are more closely related to scorpions and spiders than true crabs. Their blue blood is used in the production of medicines and vaccines.

Living barnacles have extra plates to seal their exoskeletons, which can be opened and closed like a door.

Titan acorn barnacle

Barnacles live permanently attached to seashore rocks, holding on with a natural glue as strong as cement. They feed with bristly feet, which emerge through a hole in their thick exoskeletons.

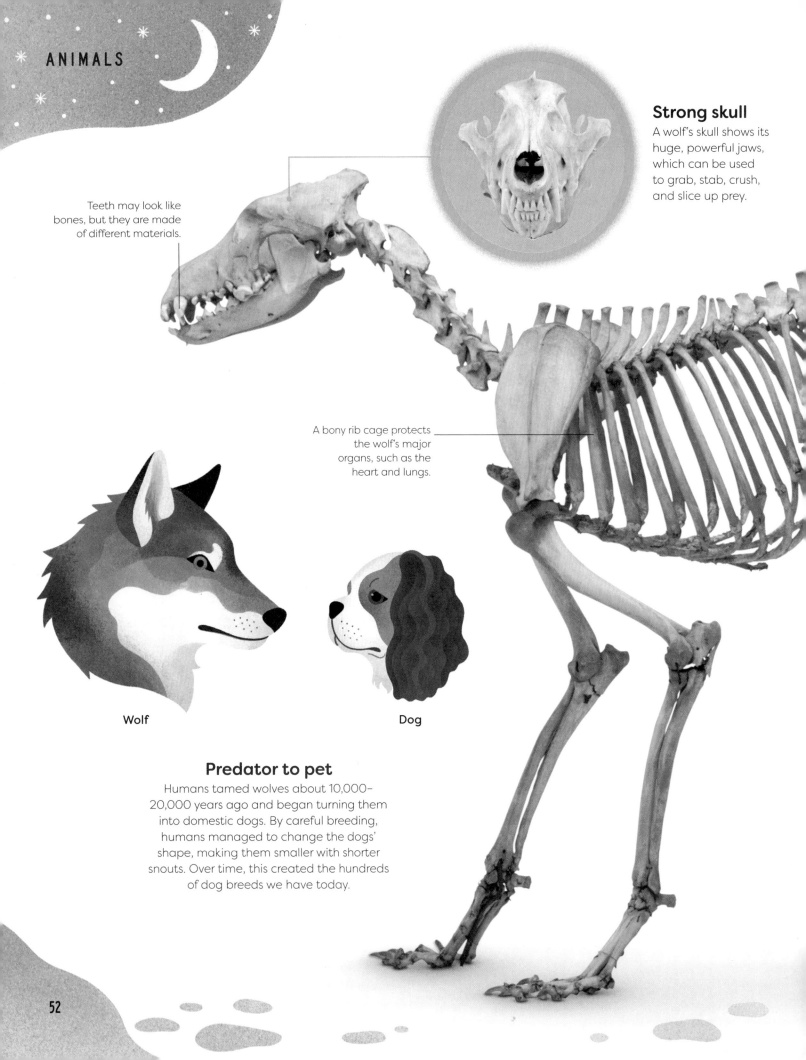

Strong skull

A wolf's skull shows its huge, powerful jaws, which can be used to grab, stab, crush, and slice up prey.

Teeth may look like bones, but they are made of different materials.

A bony rib cage protects the wolf's major organs, such as the heart and lungs.

Wolf

Dog

Predator to pet

Humans tamed wolves about 10,000–20,000 years ago and began turning them into domestic dogs. By careful breeding, humans managed to change the dogs' shape, making them smaller with shorter snouts. Over time, this created the hundreds of dog breeds we have today.

Wolf skeleton

A gray wolf's bones give it power, speed, and flexibility, making it a top predator.

Some animals have a beautiful bony skeleton. They are called vertebrates, and include mammals such as wolves as well as reptiles, amphibians, birds, and fish. All vertebrates rely on their skeleton as internal scaffolding. Without it, they would collapse in a wobbly heap! Bone is a complicated material, made from many ingredients. The main ones are a protein called collagen, which makes bone slightly bendy, and the minerals calcium and phosphate, which give strength. If comparing the same weight of each, bone is stronger than steel!

If we now look at our gray-wolf skeleton, it tells us much about how this magnificent animal lives. The skeleton is extremely strong because the wolf has to chase and catch prey. Long leg bones and a flexible spine are designed for speed. However, there is something missing—the muscles, tendons, and ligaments that hold the skeleton together and make it move. Bones, or groups of bones, are usually controlled by pairs of muscles that pull in opposite directions. The muscles position the bones as needed.

Joints in a skeleton allow it to move and bend.

Gray wolf
(Canis lupus)
Gray wolves live in the northern half of the world. By hunting in packs, they can target prey as large as caribou and bison.

Bone structure

The outside of a bone is made of a hard, smooth layer called compact bone. Under this are one of two types of jellylike bone marrow. In all vertebrates except for fish, yellow bone marrow is fatty and red bone marrow is where blood cells are made.

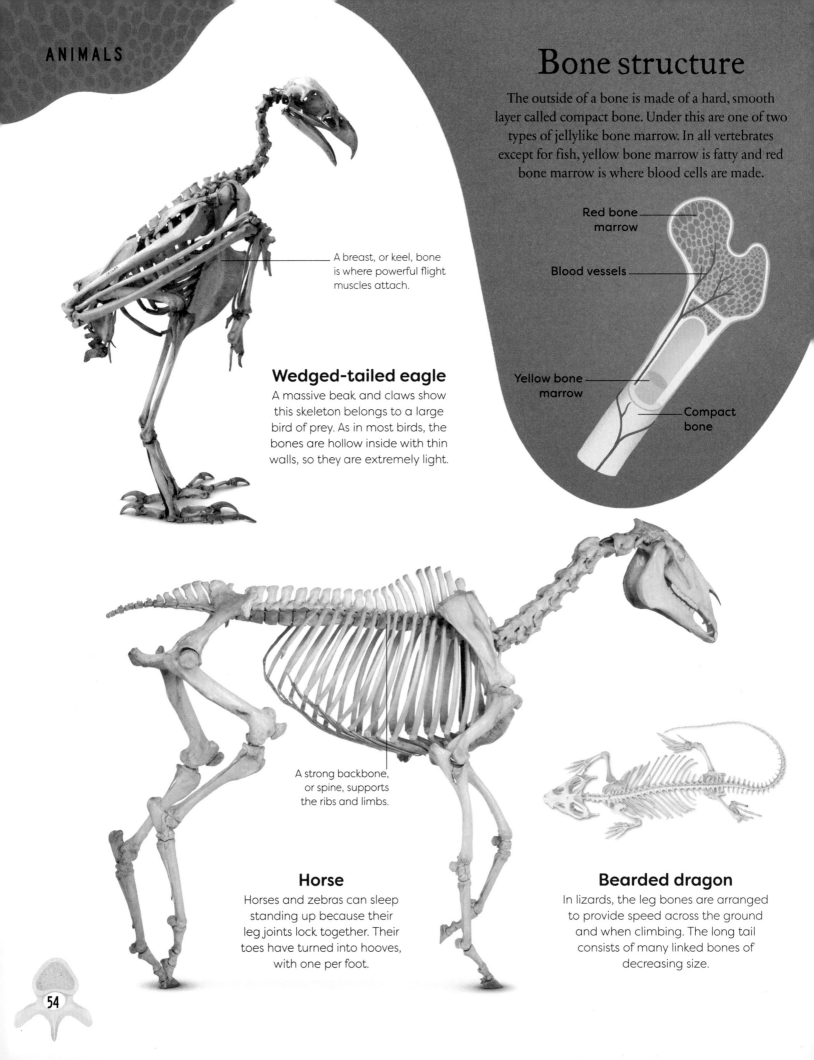

Red bone marrow

Blood vessels

Yellow bone marrow

Compact bone

A breast, or keel, bone is where powerful flight muscles attach.

Wedged-tailed eagle

A massive beak and claws show this skeleton belongs to a large bird of prey. As in most birds, the bones are hollow inside with thin walls, so they are extremely light.

A strong backbone, or spine, supports the ribs and limbs.

Horse

Horses and zebras can sleep standing up because their leg joints lock together. Their toes have turned into hooves, with one per foot.

Bearded dragon

In lizards, the leg bones are arranged to provide speed across the ground and when climbing. The long tail consists of many linked bones of decreasing size.

Vertebrate skeletons

Bones are very much alive, and they act as a frame for a vertebrate's body. Different animals have many of the same groups of bones, even though they are different shapes. For example, human arms share features with the front legs of a horse, seal flippers, and eagle wings.

Radiated tortoise

A tortoise's domed shell is made of bony plates covered in keratin. Its spine and ribs are joined to the upper shell. Its belly is protected by more bony plates, together called a plastron.

Jumping bullfrog

Bullfrogs have giant back legs for leaping around, and these need extra joints to fold up. The legs are connected to a huge hip bone and powerful leg muscles.

Galápagos penguin

Penguin arm bones have become longer and flatter, turning their wings into flippers. They are heavier and more solid than in a flying bird, which helps penguins swim deep and fast.

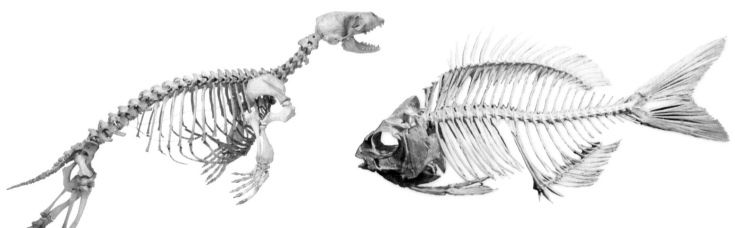

Harbor seal

Each of a seal's limbs has three joints: a shoulder or hip, an elbow or knee, and a wrist or ankle. Most other mammals have a similar arrangement, wherever they live.

Sheepshead fish

Bony fish, such as North America's sheepshead, have a long, flexible backbone down the center of their bodies. Strong spines extend from the skeleton, and these support the fins.

Antlers look like weapons, but really they are for showing off.

The paler antler tips have been polished by being rubbed on trees and the ground.

Test of strength

Stags roar and strut around to impress females. Only if the males are well matched do they clash antlers to see who is stronger.

Curved shape

Antlers are curved in such a way that the points rarely cause serious injury during battles.

Older stags have antlers with more points, known as tines.

Antlers grow directly out of the top of the skull.

Antlers

Every year, many species of deer grow a spectacular pair of bony extensions to their skulls.

In spring, if you're very lucky, you might find a freshly discarded antler while walking through the woods. Male red deer, called stags, lose their antlers between March and May and then grow a whole new set. The females, known as hinds, never grow any. In fact, of all the deer species, only female caribou grow antlers, and they aren't as spectacular as the males' antlers. Male deer use their antlers to show how strong they are.

Deer antlers are solid bone, unlike the horns of sheep, goats, and antelopes, which have a bony center with an outer layer of keratin—the same stuff our nails are made of. Another difference is that horns are permanent and keep growing throughout the animal's life, whereas antlers are grown fresh every year. Each new set of antlers is even more impressive than the previous year's, with longer branches and more forks. The oldest stags may end up carrying 33 lb (15 kg) of antler on their heads, with a dozen or more sharp points on each.

Red deer
(Cervus elaphus)
Red deer roam the forests and mountains of Europe and western Asia. A similar species, the elk, lives in North America.

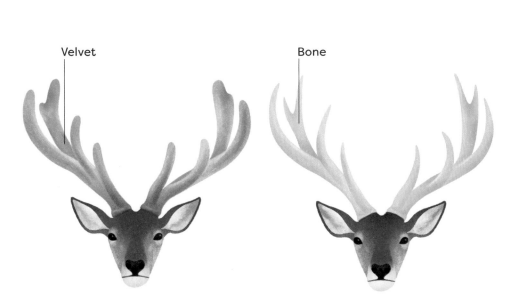

Velvet

Bone

Hairy headgear

Red deer antlers develop over the summer. They grow very quickly and are covered in gray, fuzzy skin, called velvet, which brings blood to the new bone. By fall, the antlers are fully formed and the stags rub them against trees to remove the velvet.

Squid beak

A squid has fascinating birdlike mouthparts that can bite through steel.

Nothing about a squid is ordinary. These ocean hunters are highly intelligent and swim in fast packs, they communicate with flashing colors, and their huge staring eyes are remarkably like our own. Squid have two tentacles and eight arms for catching and holding prey. Among them is hidden the lethal beak. It is as sharp as the sharpest kitchen knife and is operated by powerful muscles, so it can chop up fish and crabs at a frightening speed.

The curious thing about squid beaks is how much they look like parrot beaks. Parrots and squid have little in common, and they live totally different lives in forests and the ocean, yet their beaks are a similar shape. What sets them apart is what they are made of. A parrot beak is bone and keratin—the material in our nails—while a squid beak contains chitin, which is the substance that makes up insect skeletons. You might, if you are lucky, find a squid beak washed up on a beach. Many whales and dolphins love to feed on squid, but the tough beaks are hard to digest, so they often swim around with bellies full of them.

Long-finned squid
(Loligo forbesii)
This pinkish-brown squid is found in the Atlantic Ocean and off the north coast of Africa. It rests during the day and hunts at night.

Inside a squid
The main part of a squid's soft body is called the mantle. It contains the internal organs and is supported from the inside by a shell, the pen. Two long feeding tentacles seize prey, and the eight arms pass the food to the squid's mouth and beak.

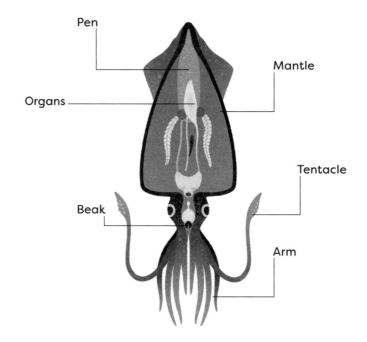

Pen

Mantle

Organs

Beak

Tentacle

Arm

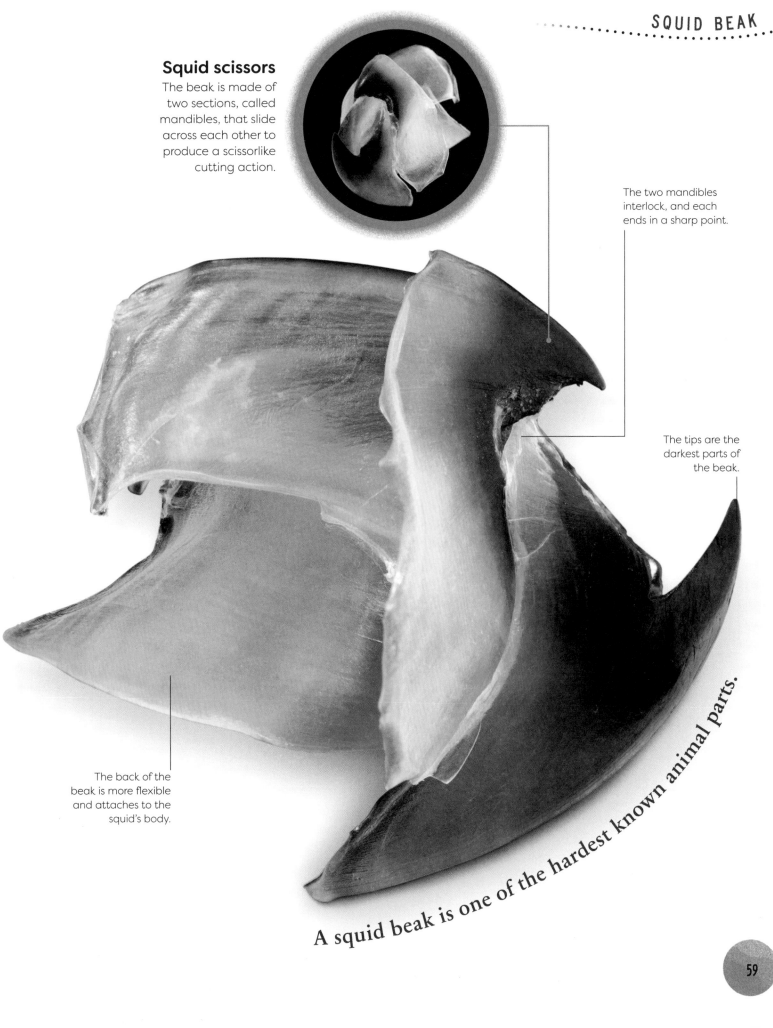

Squid scissors
The beak is made of two sections, called mandibles, that slide across each other to produce a scissorlike cutting action.

The two mandibles interlock, and each ends in a sharp point.

The tips are the darkest parts of the beak.

The back of the beak is more flexible and attaches to the squid's body.

A squid beak is one of the hardest known animal parts.

59

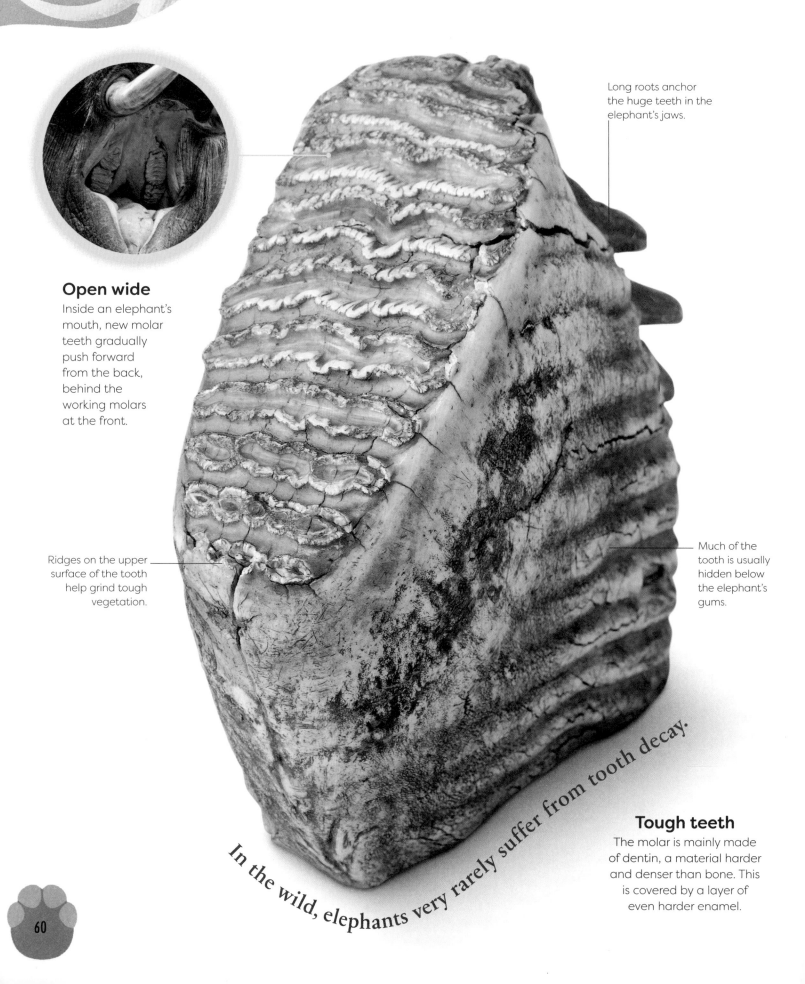

Open wide

Inside an elephant's mouth, new molar teeth gradually push forward from the back, behind the working molars at the front.

Long roots anchor the huge teeth in the elephant's jaws.

Ridges on the upper surface of the tooth help grind tough vegetation.

Much of the tooth is usually hidden below the elephant's gums.

In the wild, elephants very rarely suffer from tooth decay.

Tough teeth

The molar is mainly made of dentin, a material harder and denser than bone. This is covered by a layer of even harder enamel.

Elephant tooth

An elephant mega-molar can crush bark and branches with ease.

Everything about elephants is enormous, including their appetite. Full-grown Asian elephants can easily munch through 330 lb (150 kg) of plants each day—that's about the weight of 1,250 bananas! These herbivores spend around 16 hours a day feeding, and their diet features many tough mouthfuls, such as bamboo, bark, roots, and branches. This means their teeth have to be extremely durable.

Elephants possess just two types of teeth. They may grow a spectacular pair of upper incisors—these are the ivory tusks—and they have wide molars inside each cheek. Each molar can weigh 4 lb (2 kg) and looks like a chunk of concrete. They do the real work of grinding and crushing food and are probably the most heavy-duty teeth in the entire animal kingdom. Only four molars are in use at any time, one on each side of the upper and lower jaw. As these mighty molars reach the end of their life, they begin to break up and fall out, but new molars are already waiting to replace them.

Asian elephant
(Elephas maximus)
These elephants live in southern Asia. They are slightly smaller than their African relatives, and unlike them, only the males have tusks.

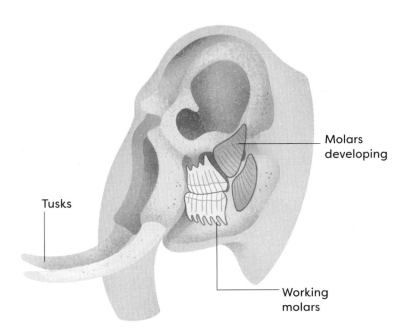

Molars developing

Tusks

Working molars

Old for new
We grow two sets of teeth in our lifetimes, but elephants swap their massive molars five times. Each new set is bigger than the one before, to keep pace with the skull as it grows. The new teeth develop at the back, ready to move forward when needed.

Teeth

The teeth of most vertebrates are made of the same materials, but they differ greatly in size and shape. Some teeth have even become fearsome tusks! Looking at teeth and skulls can tell you about the owners' diet and lifestyle.

European beaver

Beavers have chisel-like incisors for gnawing wood. These grow nonstop, as in other rodents, but wear down with daily use. The teeth are orange from the iron that strengthens the enamel.

Common dolphin

A dolphin's long jawbones have many short teeth, all the same size and shape. The teeth grip fish, but they are not used for chewing, since dolphins usually swallow their prey whole.

Horse

There is a gap between the large incisors at the front of a horse's jaw and the rows of molars farther back. Many other herbivores have a similar gap to help them chew plants.

Tiger

Tigers have two pairs of giant, curved canines, which slot into spaces outside the jaws. Of all the big cats, their canines are among the largest, reaching up to 3 in (7 cm) long.

Types of teeth

Carnivores, which mainly eat meat, have small incisors, long, sharp canines, and sharp-edged molars for slicing. Herbivores, which mainly eat plants, have big, powerful incisors, small canines—or none—and many wide, ridged molars for grinding vegetation.

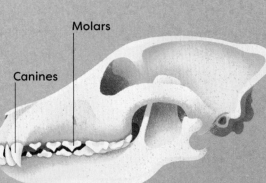

Molars

Canines

Incisors

Carnivore teeth

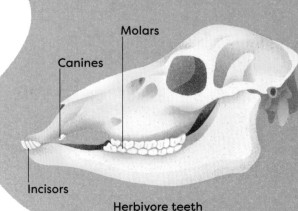

Molars

Canines

Incisors

Herbivore teeth

Aardvark

Aardvarks lick up ants and termites and as adults they only have molar teeth. These teeth are very unusual because they lack roots and enamel and keep wearing away and regrowing.

Narwhal

The male narwhal has a tusk that can grow twice as long as a pool cue. The tusk is actually a twisted upper canine, which the whale may use to sense its surroundings.

Nile crocodile

A crocodile's long jaws are packed with teeth that have the same pointed shape—perfect for gripping prey. The upper and lower teeth fit in between each other.

Eastern green mamba

Snake teeth point backward like hooks and are as sharp as needles. Venomous snakes, such as this mamba, also have long fangs at the front, with grooves for the venom to flow down.

Shark teeth

Sharks like this sand tiger constantly replace
their pointed teeth. The teeth line up in rows and
don't have roots, so they can move. When a tooth at
the front falls out, one in the row behind is pushed
forward slowly to take its place. Some sharks get
through more than 30,000 teeth during their lifetime.

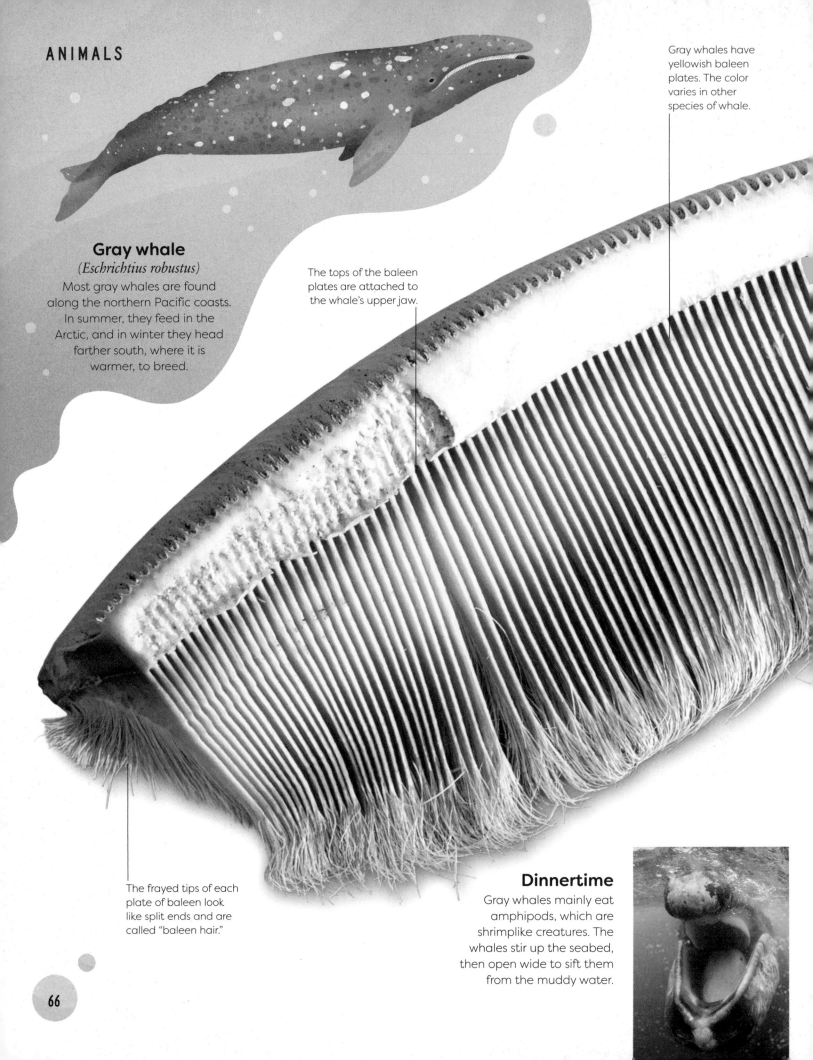

Gray whales have yellowish baleen plates. The color varies in other species of whale.

Gray whale
(*Eschrichtius robustus*)
Most gray whales are found along the northern Pacific coasts. In summer, they feed in the Arctic, and in winter they head farther south, where it is warmer, to breed.

The tops of the baleen plates are attached to the whale's upper jaw.

The frayed tips of each plate of baleen look like split ends and are called "baleen hair."

Dinnertime
Gray whales mainly eat amphipods, which are shrimplike creatures. The whales stir up the seabed, then open wide to sift them from the muddy water.

Baleen

Some whales have jaws full of bristly baleen to trap their prey.

The easiest way to fish something out of the water is with a sieve or net. This is precisely how some of the larger whales feed. Instead of teeth, they have baleen. This hangs down in parallel sheets from the whales' upper jaws. If you could touch it, it would feel like the stiff bristles of a brush. Baleen is made of the protein keratin, which is common throughout the animal kingdom, found in everything from hooves and feathers to human hair. It enables a toothless gray whale to sieve and swallow more than 2,200 lb (1,000 kg) of food daily, the equivalent of eating a full-grown giraffe!

Unfortunately, in the past, the size of whales made them a target for fleets of whaling ships, which harvested the whales' blubber (fat), meat, and baleen. The baleen was turned into many products, including hair combs, corsets (a style of women's undergarment), and the folding arms on umbrellas. In the early 1900s, however, people switched to using a new material—plastic. This contributed to the decline of whale hunting, and finally to its ban in 1986.

Parallel plates

Baleen grows in sheets, called plates. Gray whales have 260–360 plates, each about the size of a piece of letter-size paper.

Filtering food

To feed, a baleen whale first takes a monster mouthful of seawater—and any tiny creatures in it. The whale then shuts its mouth and pushes its tongue forward to force the water back out through its baleen. In the process, food items are sieved out and the whale then swallows them.

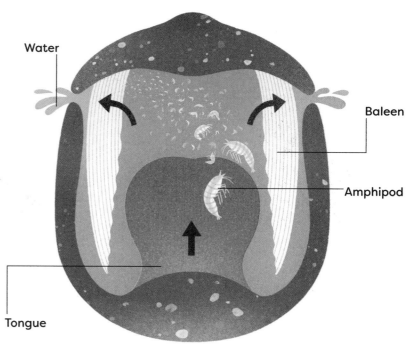

Water

Baleen

Amphipod

Tongue

A or B?

There are two main kinds of keratin, known as alpha (A) and beta (B). Type A is present in mammals, while type B is found in birds and reptiles.

Mammals

Reptiles

Crested porcupine quill

If they feel threatened, porcupines raise their long, sharp quills, which are a special type of stiff hair made of keratin. Sometimes quills come off and can be found lying on the ground.

Mouflon horn

Male mouflon, a species of wild sheep, develop a pair of magnificent curved horns. The horns, which are used for display and head-butting battles, have a bony core covered with keratin.

Radiated tortoise shell

A tortoise shell is made of bone, with an outer layer of keratin for extra strength and waterproofing. The keratin grows in patches, called scutes, which can have bold patterns on them.

Brown-throated sloth claw

These sloths have three huge claws that look like overgrown nails. In fact, they are curved bones covered in keratin. The sloths use them as climbing hooks and defensive weapons.

Keratin

Keratin is a protein that toughens skin. It also forms hair, scales, feathers, nails, claws, and hooves, and it even makes the outer part of mammal horns and bird beaks. Here are some examples of how keratin is used in the animal kingdom.

Platypus beak

Though many animals have a beak, only a few mammals do. One is the Australian platypus, whose rubbery beak consists of keratin on top of a bony extension to the skull.

Plains zebra hoof

It may not look like it, but zebras—and horses—are always standing on tiptoes! What were their middle toes have turned into solid hooves, with bones at the center and a keratin covering.

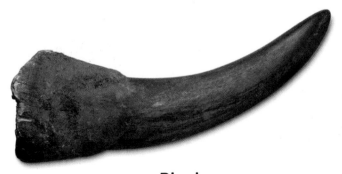

Black rhinoceros horn

Rhinoceroses use their long keratin horns to fight. However, thousands of rhinos have been killed for their horns, which some people believe work as a medicine. Black rhinos are now in danger of becoming extinct.

Western diamondback rattlesnake rattle

This rattle is made of hollow rings of keratin at the end of the snake's tail. When vibrated around 50 times a second, it makes a low-pitched buzz as a warning.

Puffin beak

The puffin has a large beak that looks different in summer and winter.

People fondly call this smart bird the "sea parrot." It is not hard to see why! During the summer breeding season, the puffin has bright orange feet and a red, yellow, and blue beak, which it uses to grab the attention of potential mates. The beak is far larger than it needs to be, but this makes it stand out even more. The puffin also uses its beak to catch fish, delicately preen its feathers, threaten rivals, and, if necessary, beak-wrestle them.

As in all birds, the puffin's beak is a bony extension of its skull. The bone has a protective cover made from keratin—a tough protein. This outer layer stores the bright pigments that give the beak its amazing colors, and it keeps growing to cope with wear and tear. The most surprising thing about puffin beaks is that every year they fall off! The whole beak is not lost, but the colorful keratin coating falls away in the fall, and a new one is regrown the following spring.

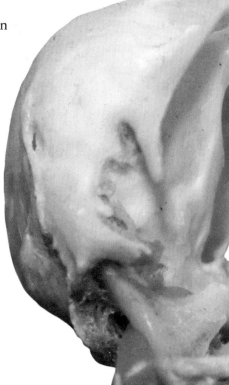

The skull has a huge opening for the eye sockets.

Summer beak

Winter beak

All change

Puffins are the only birds that change, or molt, part of their beaks. The nine panels of keratin that make it so eye-catching fall off in the fall, leaving a duller, smaller beak for the winter. Some of the puffin's feathers change color for winter, too.

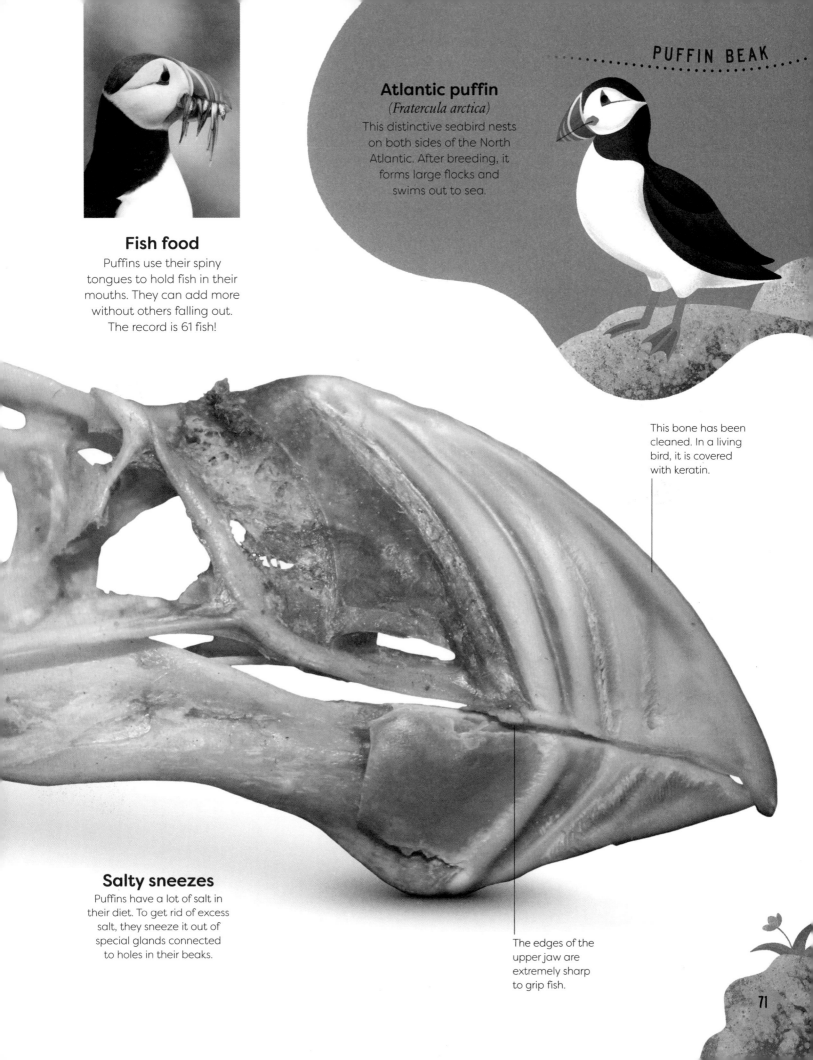

Fish food

Puffins use their spiny tongues to hold fish in their mouths. They can add more without others falling out. The record is 61 fish!

Atlantic puffin
(*Fratercula arctica*)

This distinctive seabird nests on both sides of the North Atlantic. After breeding, it forms large flocks and swims out to sea.

This bone has been cleaned. In a living bird, it is covered with keratin.

Salty sneezes

Puffins have a lot of salt in their diet. To get rid of excess salt, they sneeze it out of special glands connected to holes in their beaks.

The edges of the upper jaw are extremely sharp to grip fish.

Beaks

In birds, the beak and skull are joined permanently. They form part of the skeleton. When the bird is alive a covering of tough keratin may make its beak brightly colored. Beaks look so different it is usually possible to figure out which species of bird they belong to.

Rhinoceros hornbill

The male rhinoceros hornbill has an enormous colorful structure above its beak. It looks a little like a rhino horn, but it is hollow and may boost the volume of his calls.

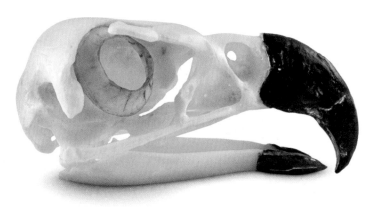

Harpy eagle

The monster beak of this rain forest eagle would fill the palm of your hand! It is as sharp as a butcher's knife, to cut up the eagle's monkey and sloth prey.

American crow

An American crow will eat most things. It relies on a strong beak that can deal with a variety of foods, from small prey to garbage left outside by humans.

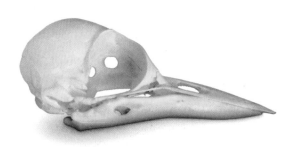

Green woodpecker

Woodpeckers hammer bark so hard they need a reinforced skull. The blows are cushioned by spongy material at the base of the beak. The birds chip holes in tree trunks for use as nests.

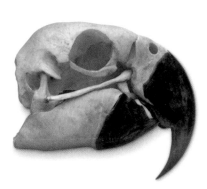

Blue-and-yellow macaw

This huge South American parrot uses its hooked beak to crack nuts and hard-shelled fruit. Yet its beak can also be very delicate when grooming its feathers.

Northern shoveler
The shoveler has a shovel-shaped beak with thin comblike "teeth" along the edges. The comb traps small animal prey as the duck sweeps its beak through the water.

Eurasian curlew
The curlew's downcurved beak is as long as a banana but much thinner. The bird pushes it deep in mud or soil to feel for worms and other burrowing animals.

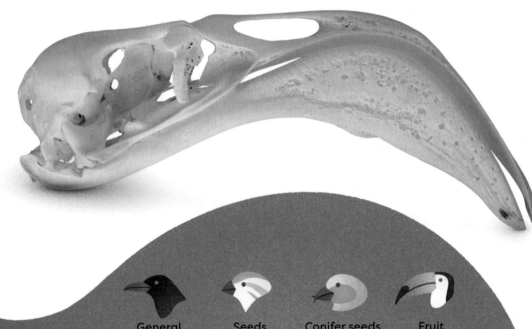

Greater flamingo
A flamingo only ever feeds with its head and beak held upside down! When it stands in this position, its beak can sift small shrimp and plantlike algae from shallow water.

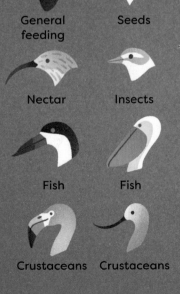

Types of beak

The shape of a bird's beak gives you a good idea of its diet. Some birds are general feeders, so they have an all-purpose beak. Others have a beak adapted for eating one type of food.

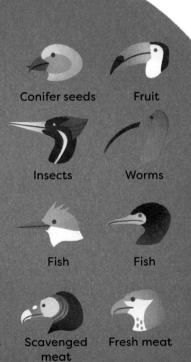

General feeding

Seeds

Conifer seeds

Fruit

Nectar

Insects

Insects

Worms

Fish

Fish

Fish

Fish

Crustaceans

Crustaceans

Scavenged meat

Fresh meat

73

CHAPTER 2

Plants,
fungi, and algae

Earth is a planet of plants, which flourish just about anywhere, from parched deserts and shallow seas to cracks in the sidewalk. Their leaves, flowers, stems, fruits, and seeds come in an incredible range of shapes, sizes, colors, and textures. Parts of fungi, such as mushrooms, and algae, such as seaweed, look very plantlike, but they belong to different groups.

Fall leaf

As summer turns to fall, sugar maples put on a spellbinding color show.

Leaves are for harvesting light energy from the sun to make food. They are like solar-powered sugar factories. The sugar production process, called photosynthesis, relies on the chemical chlorophyll, which is bright green. This is why so many trees and plants have green leaves. Photosynthesis becomes less effective when sunlight levels decline. When fall arrives in cooler parts of the world, such as North America's maple forests, deciduous trees, including the sugar maple, stop the process until spring. They break down the unwanted chlorophyll and drop their leaves.

When the green chlorophyll is gone, other colorful pigments—which were always there—are revealed. Pigments called xanthophylls, also found in egg yolks, turn maple leaves yellow. Carotenes, also found in carrots, turn them orange. However, the most dramatic change is still to come. Any sugar left in the maple leaves is converted into anthocyanins. These pigments, which also occur in cherries, strawberries, and beets, turn the leaves brilliant red and purple. The display lasts for just a few weeks and then the leaves start to die. One by one, their colors fade and they fall to the ground.

Sugar maple
(Acer saccharum)
Sugar maples grow in the southeast of Canada and the northeast of the USA, where their golden sap is processed to make sweet maple syrup.

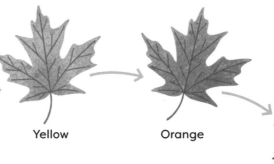

Light green

Yellow

Orange

Red

Green

Rainbow leaves
When a maple leaf's green chlorophyll fades away, it allows other yellow and orange pigments in the leaf to be seen. Until this point, the chlorophyll hides these colors. Red and purple appear next, and when the leaf dies, it turns brown.

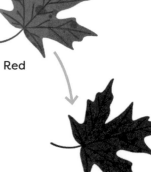

Brown

Frosty nights and sunny days make maple leaves even redder.

Red is always one of the last shades to appear.

Maple leaves have points, like a hand with outstretched fingers.

Each leaf changes color gradually, and it may be more than one color at a time.

Fading fast

After they drop, maple leaves dry out and become brittle. Their bright fall tints fade and they turn brown and crispy.

Patchy color

Sugar maples may not change color evenly, because some parts of the tree receive more sunlight than others.

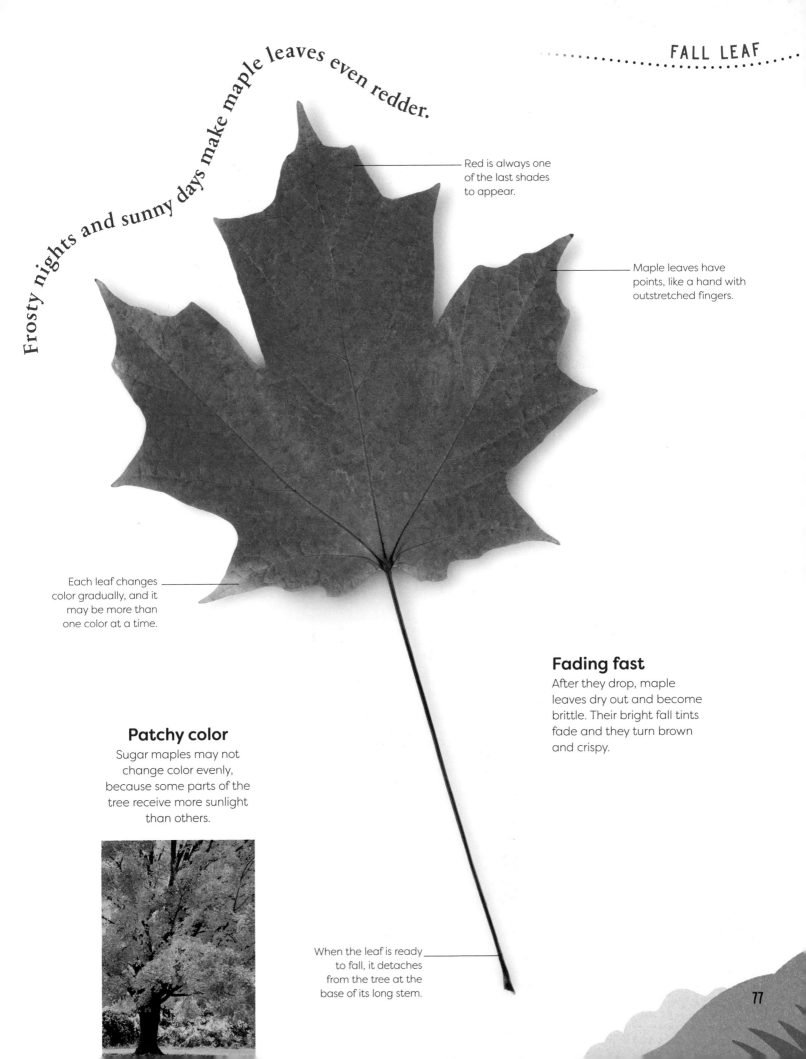

When the leaf is ready to fall, it detaches from the tree at the base of its long stem.

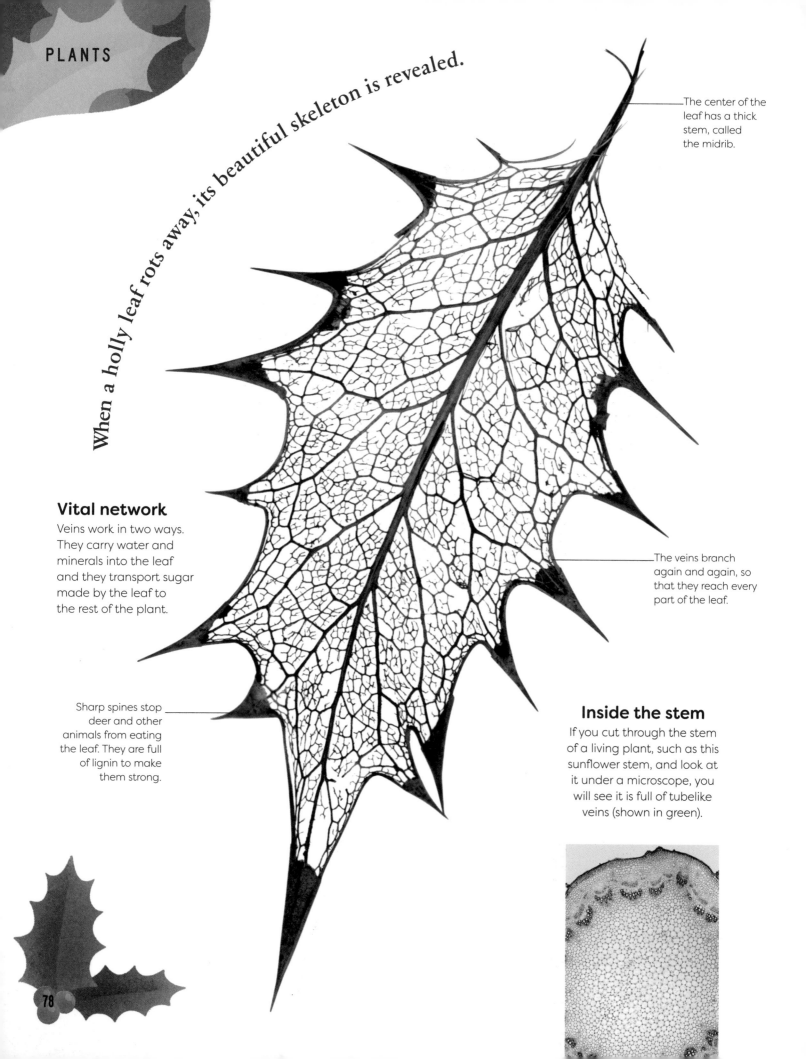

When a holly leaf rots away, its beautiful skeleton is revealed.

The center of the leaf has a thick stem, called the midrib.

Vital network

Veins work in two ways. They carry water and minerals into the leaf and they transport sugar made by the leaf to the rest of the plant.

The veins branch again and again, so that they reach every part of the leaf.

Sharp spines stop deer and other animals from eating the leaf. They are full of lignin to make them strong.

Inside the stem

If you cut through the stem of a living plant, such as this sunflower stem, and look at it under a microscope, you will see it is full of tubelike veins (shown in green).

Leaf skeleton

Every leaf has a skeleton, but it is made up of an intricate pattern of veins, rather than bones.

Underneath a tree you will often find a carpet of dead leaves, which may be crunchy or soggy, depending on whether it has rained. This leafy layer, called leaf litter, makes a superb habitat for all kinds of small creatures—from busy beetles to many-legged millipedes. Before long, the fallen leaves start to decay and turn to mush, which adds nutrients to the soil. However, some leaves—such as holly—do not disappear entirely. The glossy green parts of a holly leaf slowly rot away, but a tough brown skeleton is left behind. The skeleton contains a stiff material called lignin, which is also found in wood and bark and lasts a long time. The skeleton forms a perfect outline of the original leaf, together with a beautiful arrangement of tubelike veins.

The leaf's veins are mostly hidden when it is still alive, and they have a vital job to do. They are part of the holly tree's internal transportation system, which reaches from its deepest roots to its highest leaves and carries the food and water that the tree needs to grow.

European holly
(Ilex aquifolium)
Holly has prickly green leaves all year round and bright red berries in winter. As its name suggests, European holly is found mostly in Europe.

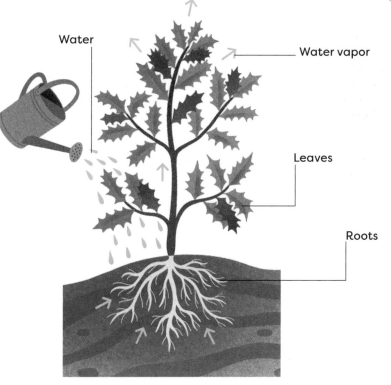

Water

Water vapor

Leaves

Roots

Water transportation
The holly tree sucks up water from the soil with its roots. The water moves up the stem and into the leaves through the veins. Water is needed for photosynthesis—the process the plant uses to make food. Any water left over escapes into the air as water vapor.

79

Leaves

We live on a green planet. Leaves of one sort or another are all around us, from the grass at our feet to the fresh foliage at the tops of the tallest trees. They vary hugely in size, shape, and texture to suit their growing conditions.

Copper beech

Leaves aren't always green! This unusual variety of the European beech tree is grown for its purplish-brown foliage. It is often planted in parks and gardens.

Veitch's pitcher plant

A single modified leaf forms a tall, slippery jug in this carnivorous plant. Insects fall into the leaf, which acts as a trap, and drown in a pool of digestive nectar at the bottom.

Nordmann fir

Waxy needles allow fir trees to store water in cold or dry conditions. They may be familiar because millions of Nordmann fir saplings are sold each year as Christmas trees.

Windmill palm

The giant leaves of this Chinese tree have many stiff leaflets that spread into a fan. Around the world, palm leaves are dried for use as roofing material.

Bracken

Bracken is a type of fern with delicate leaves called fronds. Each frond is rolled up when it erupts from the ground. It then unfurls to reveal its symmetrical pattern of leaflets.

Welwitschia

This desert plant from Namibia only ever has two leaves. They keep growing for the lifetime of the plant and shred into long ribbons. Some welwitschia can be 1,500 years old!

Leaf types

Deciduous trees drop all their leaves in winter or during dry periods. By contrast, evergreen trees keep their leaves all year and replace them infrequently. Evergreen trees include most conifers, which have needle-shaped leaves.

Deciduous

Evergreen

Houseleek leaves are fat and fleshy, with a smooth surface.

Houseleek

The curious leaves of houseleeks have no obvious stem. They store as much water as possible so they can cope with long periods without rain.

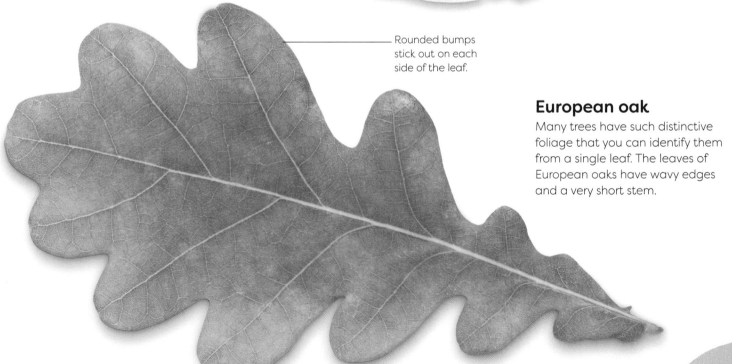

Rounded bumps stick out on each side of the leaf.

European oak

Many trees have such distinctive foliage that you can identify them from a single leaf. The leaves of European oaks have wavy edges and a very short stem.

Cactus spines

Cacti are covered in vicious spines, a special kind of leaf in which the cells have died and hardened. They can be brutally sharp, as in this prickly pear cactus, which is sometimes planted as an animal-proof hedge. The spines guard the precious water stored inside the swollen stems of this desert plant.

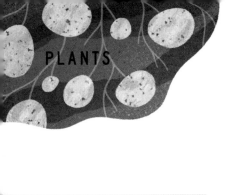

Potatoes are covered in spots known as "eyes."

Ancient potatoes had yellow flesh and dark purple skin.

Ready to sprout

Potatoes have eyes, but they can't see. These dimples are actually the places from which the pale roots and shoots of new potato plants may grow.

Tough, colorful potato skin protects the starchy flesh inside.

A potato stays firm and fresh as long as it is in the ground.

Many colors

Today's potatoes can be brown, yellow, pink, purple, or red. The flesh is usually white, yellow, or pinkish. If exposed to sunlight, the potato can turn green and is then poisonous, even when cooked.

Potato

Familiar all over the world, this vegetable is a food store for the potato plant.

Potatoes have played a major part in human history. Over the centuries, people have bred hundreds of different varieties—large and small, smooth and knobby, fat and finger-thin, with skins in rainbow colors and a taste from nutty to sweet. In South America, archeologists have found the earliest evidence of potatoes being grown as a crop. At least 8,000 years ago, in the high Andes mountains of Peru, people were planting them with simple tools such as digging sticks. Later, potatoes fed the cities and armies of the mighty Inca empire. The Incas even worshiped a potato goddess named Axomamma.

What exactly is a potato, though? It looks like part of the plant's roots, but, in fact, it is a massively swollen underground stem called a tuber. The potato plant fills the tuber with supplies of food, so it can survive cold winters and long droughts. If left in the soil unharvested, the potato may sprout and grow into a new plant. Potatoes are a popular food, so it may be a surprise to learn that all parts of the potato plant except the tubers are poisonous.

Potato plant
(Solanum tuberosum)
The potato plants we grow have dozens of wild relatives in South America, which look similar but produce smaller potatoes.

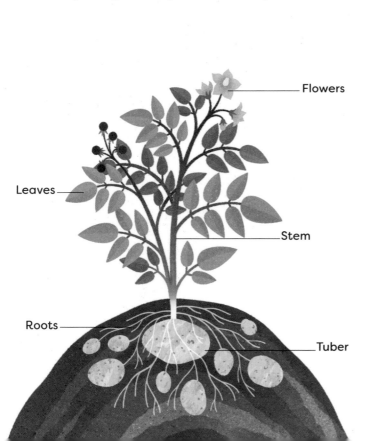

Flowers

Leaves

Stem

Roots

Tuber

Energy store

As it matures, a potato plant develops more and more tubers at the base of its roots. The tubers act as energy reserves. A potato tuber is one-fifth starch, a type of carbohydrate, and four-fifths water.

Larva — 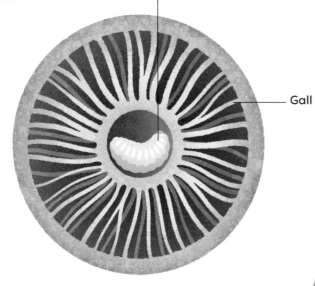 — Gall

Safe nursery

To begin with, the gall is soft and green, but over the summer it turns hard and brown. It is full of spongelike padding, which surrounds a central chamber. This is the snug home of a single gall wasp larva.

Minibeast

Few people have seen the oak marble gall wasp because it is just 0.06 in (1.5 mm) long.

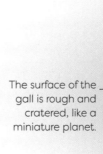

The surface of the gall is rough and cratered, like a miniature planet.

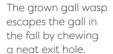

The grown gall wasp escapes the gall in the fall by chewing a neat exit hole.

Oak gall

A tiny wasp injects an oak tree with chemicals to create the perfect nursery for its larva.

Small creatures can have a big impact. There is a wasp that is barely large enough for us to see, yet it somehow takes control of a mighty oak tree. Meet the oak marble gall wasp. In spring, the female wasp lays her eggs in the leaf buds of oaks. At the same time, she injects a cocktail of chemicals. These cause the buds to grow in an odd way. Instead of developing into normal leaves, each bud forms a small ball called an oak marble gall, which acts as a nursery for a single wasp larva. Safe inside, the larva feeds on the oak until it is ready to change into an adult. There are many other gall wasps, some of which also target oaks, and others that prefer different plants and trees. All produce galls of different shapes, sizes, and colors.

Oak marble galls are particularly important because for more than 1,300 years, they were gathered to make black ink. Gall ink was used to write some of the world's most famous documents, including the Magna Carta in 1215, the US Constitution in 1789, and the oldest surviving copy of the Bible.

Oak tree
(*Quercus*)
Several types of oak tree in Europe are targeted by oak marble gall wasps, including the common oak.

Hidden moths

The gray moths that the larvae turn into are hardly ever seen because they are so small and well camouflaged.

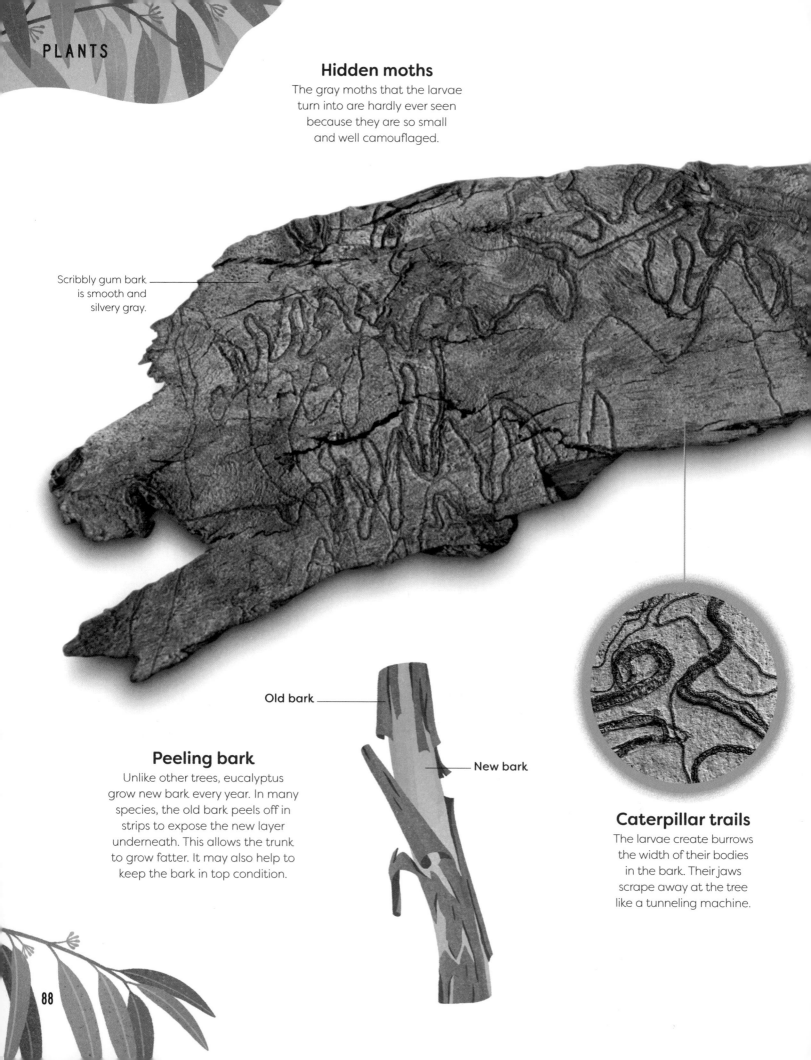

Scribbly gum bark is smooth and silvery gray.

Old bark

New bark

Peeling bark

Unlike other trees, eucalyptus grow new bark every year. In many species, the old bark peels off in strips to expose the new layer underneath. This allows the trunk to grow fatter. It may also help to keep the bark in top condition.

Caterpillar trails

The larvae create burrows the width of their bodies in the bark. Their jaws scrape away at the tree like a tunneling machine.

Squiggles show the route taken by the feeding larvae.

Eucalyptus bark

Strange scribbles dug into this bark are the work of insect larvae.

In a hot and dry Australian woodland, there is a tree with loops, squiggles, and zigzags all over its bark. It is a eucalyptus tree, and the marks look just like doodles. Other eucalyptus trees nearby are also covered in these patterns. All are unique. Have messages been scratched into the bark? Surely a person did this? In fact, there is no doubt about the identity of the doodler, or rather, doodlers. They are small white insect larvae, no bigger than a grain of rice. Eventually, the wormlike larvae will turn into moths. First, though, they spend many months eating bark and growing. Their nonstop bark munching creates the patterns, which stay hidden until the outer layer of eucalyptus bark peels away.

These particular moth larvae always scribble on the same species of eucalyptus, or gum, tree. No other tree will do. Its name is, obviously, the scribbly gum! In other parts of the world, too, unusual doodles appear on bark and leaves, and even inside the wood at the center of tree trunks. These are created by different insects, mostly the larvae of moths and beetles.

Scribbly gum
(Eucalyptus haemastoma)
Three-quarters of the trees in Australia are eucalyptus (gum) trees. Scribbly gums are from the area around the city of Sydney.

89

Some flowers may only bloom for a single day.

Nectar guides
Insects can detect ultraviolet light that we can't see. This daisy has markings that are invisible to us, but that guide insects to their nectar.

Many flowers
Flowers in the dandelion family have a secret. They are actually a cluster of many small flowers called florets. Here each floret has a single pink petal.

The reproductive structures in the center of the dandelion are yellow and have curly ends.

The many brightly colored petals open wide to help insects land and perch.

Flower

Flowers attract attention with irresistible colors, patterns, scents, and sweet nectar.

Throughout history, flowers have been at the heart of human cultures and traditions. People have told stories and sung songs about them, used them as dye and in natural cures, and offered them as gifts and tokens of love. Flowers, however, are not here for our benefit—their real purpose is to produce seeds. The showiest flowers may look attractive to us, but they are really aimed at pollinators—including insects, birds, and even tiny mammals—which will carry the flowers' pollen between blooms.

Some flowers aim to entice a variety of pollinators, so they have a color, shape, and perfume with broad appeal. Other flowers, such as orchids, target a particular type of pollinator, or sometimes just a single species. Their flower structure allows only the chosen species to enter and keeps out the rest. Many flowers produce a sugary liquid, called nectar, deep in their center which tempts pollinators close to the pollen. Some flowers also send other signals that humans are unable to detect. Pollinators experience the world differently from us, and they see patterns and markings we cannot.

Pink dandelion
(Crepis incana)
There are hundreds of dandelion-like flowers worldwide. This unusual pink species is from the mountains of southern Greece.

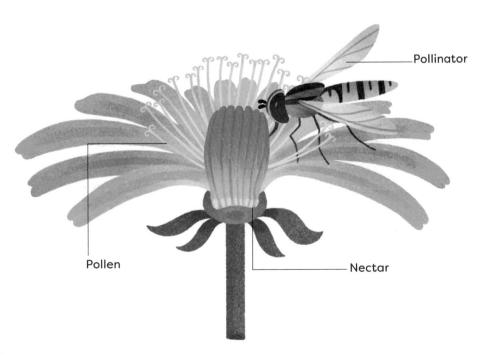

Pollinator

Pollen

Nectar

Life of a flower
Every flowering plant has a growing cycle. Pink dandelions send up fresh leaves when the spring sun warms the mountain soil. They flower in summer to attract a variety of insects, including bees, hoverflies, and butterflies, to name just a few. After flowering, the dandelions produce seeds.

Flowers

The Earth would be a much duller place without flowers. Scientists have identified around 370,000 species of flowering plants, and more are discovered every year. Their blooms may be wider than a doorway or as small as the periods in this book.

Banana

Clusters of banana flowers are hidden under special purple leaves. Eventually, the flowers turn into the familiar yellow fruit. In southern Asia, banana blossom is a common cooking ingredient.

Bird of paradise

This South African flower has a curious pollination strategy. When nectar-eating birds visit, they receive a dusting of pollen on their feet. This rubs off on the next flower on which they land.

Bee orchid

Many orchids look like insects, and this species looks just like a female bee. Male bees are attracted to the orchid, but they have been tricked and become covered in pollen.

Bougainvillea

It is not petals that give this climbing plant its gorgeous color but leafy structures, called bracts. The actual petals are white and barely noticeable.

Sunflower

Within 90 days of a seed being planted, a sunflower's golden head may tower several yards above the ground. Wild ones are far smaller and don't grow so fast.

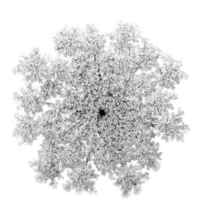

Wild carrot

This frilly flower smells of carrots, since it is the ancestor of the root vegetable we eat today. Many plants have similar dense heads of white flowers, known as umbels.

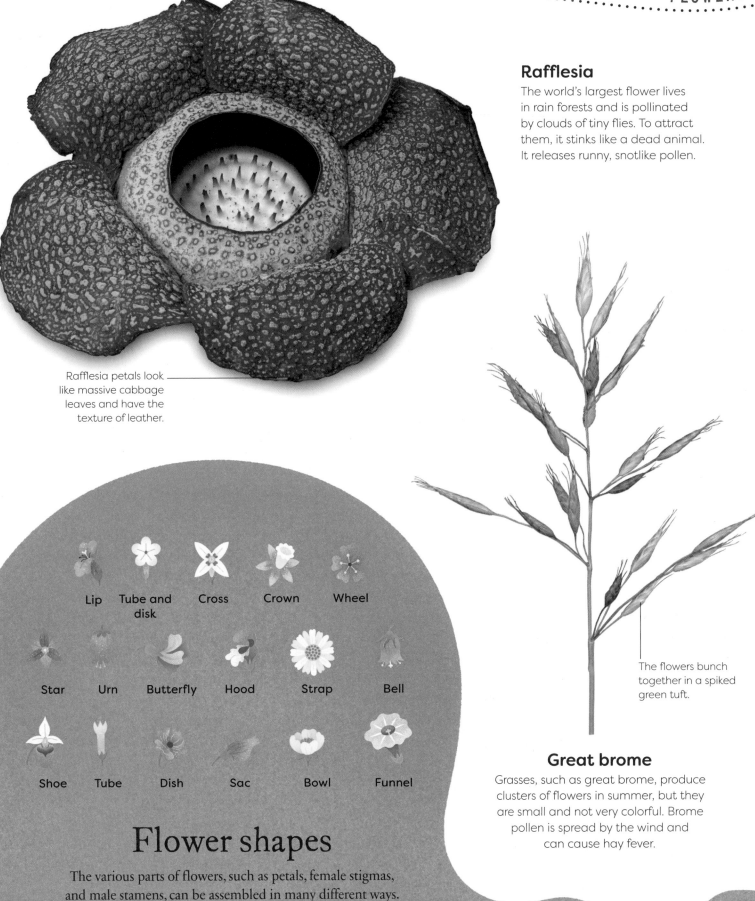

Rafflesia

The world's largest flower lives in rain forests and is pollinated by clouds of tiny flies. To attract them, it stinks like a dead animal. It releases runny, snotlike pollen.

Rafflesia petals look like massive cabbage leaves and have the texture of leather.

The flowers bunch together in a spiked green tuft.

Great brome

Grasses, such as great brome, produce clusters of flowers in summer, but they are small and not very colorful. Brome pollen is spread by the wind and can cause hay fever.

Lip   Tube and disk   Cross   Crown   Wheel

Star   Urn   Butterfly   Hood   Strap   Bell

Shoe   Tube   Dish   Sac   Bowl   Funnel

Flower shapes

The various parts of flowers, such as petals, female stigmas, and male stamens, can be assembled in many different ways. Each type of arrangement is suited to different pollinators.

Pollinator at work

This bumblebee is causing quite a buzz. By beating its wings around 200 times a second, it creates vibrations that shake sunflower pollen onto its furry body. Buzz pollination is hard work, but also highly effective. The bumblebee's reward is to become covered in sticky, nutritious pollen.

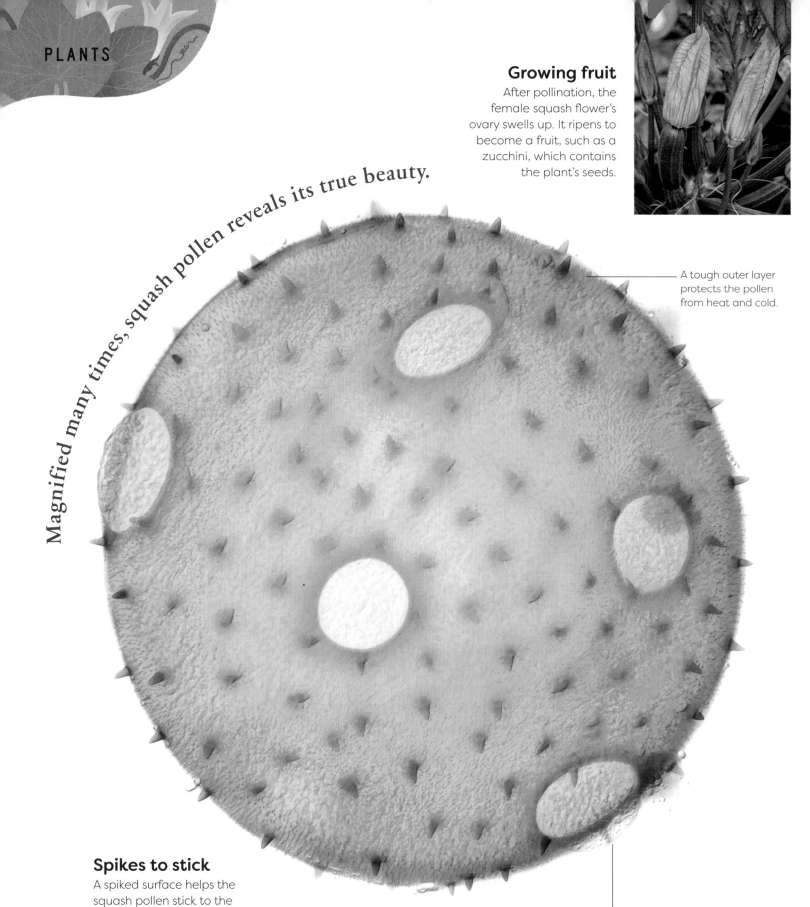

Growing fruit
After pollination, the female squash flower's ovary swells up. It ripens to become a fruit, such as a zucchini, which contains the plant's seeds.

Magnified many times, squash pollen reveals its true beauty.

A tough outer layer protects the pollen from heat and cold.

Spikes to stick
A spiked surface helps the squash pollen stick to the hairy bodies and legs of insect pollinators such as bees.

Holes in the pollen's surface allow the reproductive cell inside to grow out to meet the ovary of a female flower.

Pollen grain

Pollen is a dustlike material that flowering plants use to reproduce.

Every flowering plant makes pollen, as do some other plants, including conifers. All pollen has a shape unique to each plant. Some grains of pollen are round like miniature peas. Others are more like footballs, bowls, or cushions. This pollen grain from a squash looks like a spiked golden sun. All pollen grains are too small for us to see individually, yet these tiny packages are essential to flowering plants, including many important crops.

Pollen is produced by the male part of a plant, and inside each grain is a single male reproductive cell. When this reaches the female parts of a plant of the same species, pollination takes place. Animals that transfer pollen are called pollinators. Insects are great at it, but many others do it, too, including birds, bats, monkeys, lemurs, and even a few lizards. Many trees and grasses use the wind for pollination, so their pollen grains have to be the smallest and lightest of all. Yet despite this, pollen is extremely tough and it can be preserved in fossils and ice. Scientists study ancient pollen to discover what plants were growing long ago.

Summer squash
(*Cucurbita pepo*)
Popular with gardeners, this North American plant produces large edible fruit in the summer. Some varieties produce zucchini, others grow squashes or pumpkins.

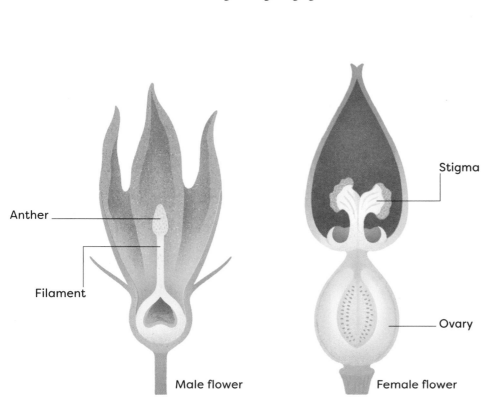

Anther

Filament

Stigma

Ovary

Male flower

Female flower

Pollen's journey
Squash pollen is released by the anther in the male flower. For pollination to occur, it must be carried to a female flower, where it sticks to the stigma. The pollen grain then grows down to reach the ovary, which turns into a fruit containing seeds.

97

Cotton boll

Fleecy bundles around the seeds of the cotton plant are the source of a wonderful natural fiber.

When a cotton plant is ready to harvest, it is covered in balls of white fluff, a little like sheep's wool or cotton candy. This fluff is the natural protective packaging around the cotton seeds. The fluff-containing seed pods, known as cotton bolls, are actually an unusual type of fruit, and they have changed the world. Can you imagine a life without cotton? It is the planet's most popular material for clothing, towels, and bedsheets, and it can be spun into many different forms, from tough denim to soft velvet. It is also used to make bandages, toothpaste, money, and explosives! Tiny scraps of old fabric show that people have been wearing cotton clothes for at least 6,000 years. The reason cotton is so popular is because it is easy to spin and dye and the cloth it produces is soft, light, and breathable.

Unfortunately, cotton is often grown using huge amounts of pesticides—which kill insects that eat the plants—and lots of water. Now, more farms are producing organic cotton, which avoids the use of chemicals, is better for the soil, and uses less water.

Fluffy ball
A boll has tens of thousands of cotton fibers in it. Each is just an inch or so long.

Cotton plant
(Gossypium)
Once, cotton grew wild in the warm parts of Africa, Asia, North America, and South America. Today, most cotton is grown on farms.

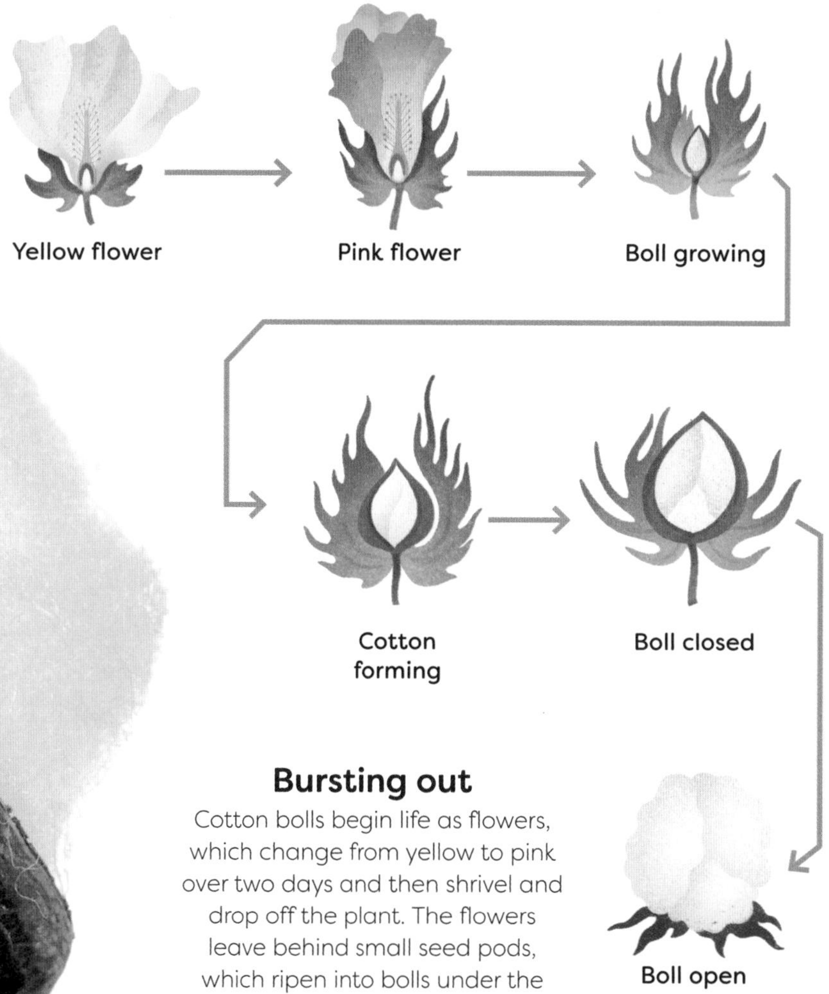

Yellow flower → Pink flower → Boll growing

Cotton forming → Boll closed

Boll open

Bursting out

Cotton bolls begin life as flowers, which change from yellow to pink over two days and then shrivel and drop off the plant. The flowers leave behind small seed pods, which ripen into bolls under the hot sun. After four months, the white bolls burst open.

Seed security

There are up to 45 seeds hidden inside a cotton boll, to which all the fuzzy cotton fibers are attached.

Every individual fiber is actually a hollow tube.

The outer part of the seed pod is hard and woody.

Cocoa pod

The seeds in this heavy, bright-red fruit are what we use to make chocolate.

Many people would not recognize a cocoa pod, yet this is where we get one of the world's favorite foods—chocolate! The pod is the fruit of the cocoa tree, which grows wild in the Amazon rain forest and on farms in the forests of West Africa, where the warm, damp, and shady conditions are ideal. How do cocoa pods form? First, flowers appear on the tree. They are tiny, so they need tiny pollinators. The minuscule chocolate midge is just the right size. For every thousand flowers that these midges pollinate, however, just two or three become cocoa pods. One pod grows from each flower and as it ripens, it often changes color from green to yellow to red.

At harvesttime, the pods' seeds are removed and roasted, which changes them from white to brown. We now call them cocoa beans, from which cocoa powder and chocolate can be made. Cocoa beans have been eaten for around 4,000 years. The Aztec people from Mexico made a bitter drink from them. To the Aztecs, cocoa was a gift from the gods—and cocoa's scientific name, Theobroma, means "food of the gods."

Cocoa tree
(Theobroma cacao)
The cocoa tree is from the tropical parts of the Americas. Its pods grow straight out of the bark of its branches and trunk.

Roasted bean

Seeds surrounded by pulp

Pod cut in half

Inside the pod
Up to 50 white seeds are packed inside a cocoa pod's tough skin. These are surrounded by a gooey white pulp that monkeys, rodents, and fruit bats all love to eat.

Midge magnet

The chocolate midges that visit cocoa flowers to sip their nectar are mostly male. The female midges bite and prefer blood.

A cocoa tree produces no more than 250 pods over its life.

The ripe pods are usually red, but can also be yellow or purple.

Hard shell

When ripe, cocoa pods develop a thick skin. Large pods are the size and shape of footballs.

Ridges run from the stalk to the tip of the pod.

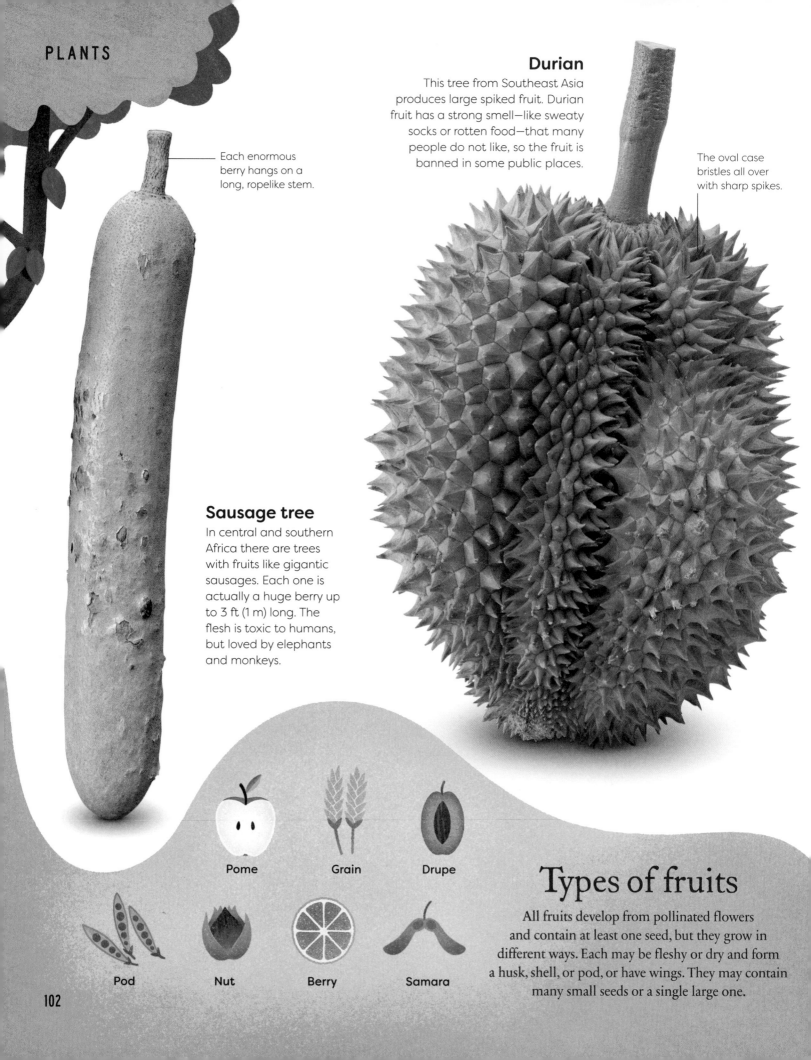

Each enormous berry hangs on a long, ropelike stem.

Durian

This tree from Southeast Asia produces large spiked fruit. Durian fruit has a strong smell—like sweaty socks or rotten food—that many people do not like, so the fruit is banned in some public places.

The oval case bristles all over with sharp spikes.

Sausage tree

In central and southern Africa there are trees with fruits like gigantic sausages. Each one is actually a huge berry up to 3 ft (1 m) long. The flesh is toxic to humans, but loved by elephants and monkeys.

Pome

Grain

Drupe

Types of fruits

All fruits develop from pollinated flowers and contain at least one seed, but they grow in different ways. Each may be fleshy or dry and form a husk, shell, or pod, or have wings. They may contain many small seeds or a single large one.

Pod

Nut

Berry

Samara

Fruits

Many fruits look, taste, and smell so tempting animals eagerly eat them, which helps spread the seeds inside. When ripe, fruits are often colorful and sugary, with sweetly scented flesh, but some are hard, dry, sour, or stinky! Nevertheless, most fruits have an animal that likes to eat them.

Pea
The pod in which green peas develop is, in fact, a fruit. Inside the pod, each pea is attached by a thread which dries and breaks easily when the pod is ripe.

Strawberry
A strawberry is not actually a fruit itself. The tiny yellow specks on the outside are each a dry fruit containing a seed, all stuck onto the red flesh.

Crimson-leaved maple
In the fall, maple trees produce hard fruits called keys. Each key has a pair of seeds attached to wings to help it fly. It whirls through the air like a helicopter.

Sweet chestnut
The sweet chestnut tree produces fruits inside very spiked green cases. The glossy brown fruit has a hard shell with a single seed inside. These types of fruits are called nuts.

Marble fruit
Years after they are picked, these clusters of small berrylike fruits from central Africa are still a bright blue. Scientists have discovered that the color is the brightest made by any plant or animal.

Cashew tree
Cashew trees, from Brazil, produce something called a cashew apple. This is a false fruit, since it is actually a swollen stem. Hanging off the bottom is the real fruit containing the cashew seed.

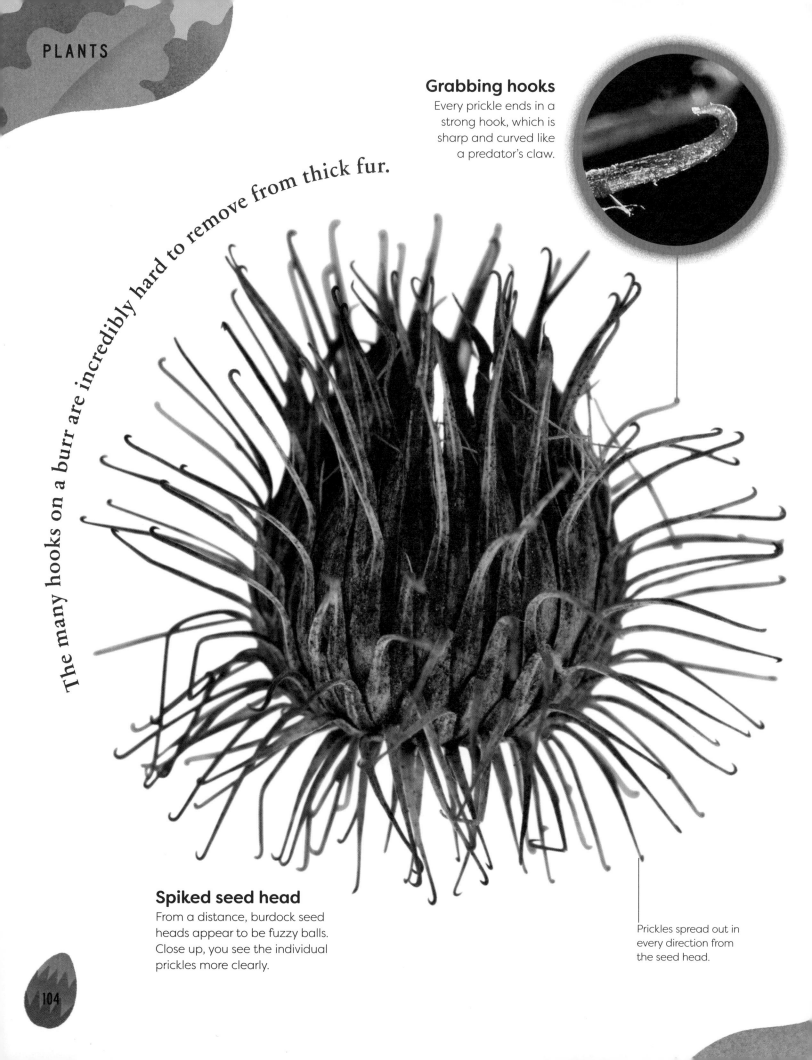

Grabbing hooks
Every prickle ends in a strong hook, which is sharp and curved like a predator's claw.

The many hooks on a burr are incredibly hard to remove from thick fur.

Spiked seed head
From a distance, burdock seed heads appear to be fuzzy balls. Close up, you see the individual prickles more clearly.

Prickles spread out in every direction from the seed head.

Burdock burr

Curved hooks enable these seed heads to cling to anything hairy that touches them.

Some plants are stickier than others, and burdock is as sticky as can be, but in a different way to glue. Burdock spends its first year growing, then in its second year it produces tuftlike purple flowers. At the end of summer, the flowers die, dry out, and turn into prickly seed containers known as burrs. These hook onto the fur of any mammal that happens to brush past them. Eventually, the burrs work loose and fall to the ground, which is how the plant spreads its seeds. Burdock burrs cling to clothing, too, so it is worth checking your coat after a walk in the countryside to see if any have become attached to it!

Burdock burrs also inspired a great invention. In 1941, the Swiss engineer George de Mestral and his dog were left covered in them after a hike. When de Mestral looked at the burrs under a microscope, he saw their hooklike structure and this gave him the idea for a new type of fastening, which he later marketed under the VELCRO® brand.

Burdock
(Arctium)
Burdock plants belong to the thistle family. They like woodland and rough ground and grow across Asia and Europe.

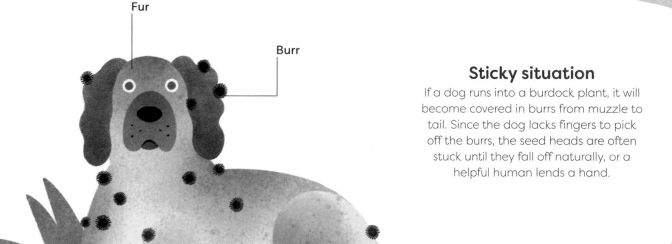

Fur

Burr

Sticky situation
If a dog runs into a burdock plant, it will become covered in burrs from muzzle to tail. Since the dog lacks fingers to pick off the burrs, the seed heads are often stuck until they fall off naturally, or a helpful human lends a hand.

Pine cone

Pine trees have always used these heavy-duty containers to keep their seeds safe, even from dinosaurs.

A pine tree weighed down by hundreds of fat cones is a wonderful sight. The cones look and feel like wood, and, in fact, are made from similar materials, including cellulose—a strong substance found in plants. A pine cone's thick scales overlap and open out in all directions when ripe. All of these cones are female, whereas the male cones are small, soft, and tricky to spot among a pine tree's needles. Why are the female cones so tough? It could be because when pine trees first appeared on Earth more than 150 million years ago, storing seeds in a really strong container was the best way of stopping long-necked dinosaurs from eating them.

Pine cones are said to forecast the weather. If you examine their scales, you will notice that on humid days when rain is likely, the scales clamp tight to stop the cone's seeds from getting soggy. On warm, dry days the scales open up to reveal the seeds inside. The seeds of the black pine have wings that carry them away with the wind.

Black pine
(Pinus nigra)
This handsome tree is a conifer found around the Mediterranean. Many conifers are long-lived, and this one can survive for up to 500 years.

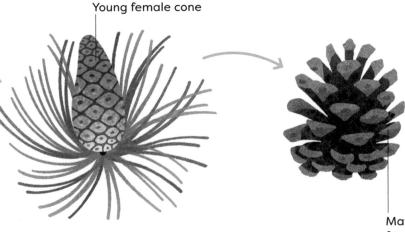

Young female cone

Mature female cone

Male cone

Growing a pine cone
In spring, tiny male cones produce dustlike pollen. The wind blows this onto larger female cones, pollinating them. As their seeds develop, the female cones grow bigger and tougher. When mature, they are hard, glossy, and brown.

Ready to fly
The seeds are deep inside the cone, nestled among the scales. Each one has a delicate wing to carry it away when the wind blows strongly enough.

Each woody scale protects two winged seeds.

The woody cones of black pines take up to three years to grow.

Spiral scales
The cone is built from spirals of woody scales. Spirals are the neatest way to pack materials into a rounded space, and they are common in nature.

107

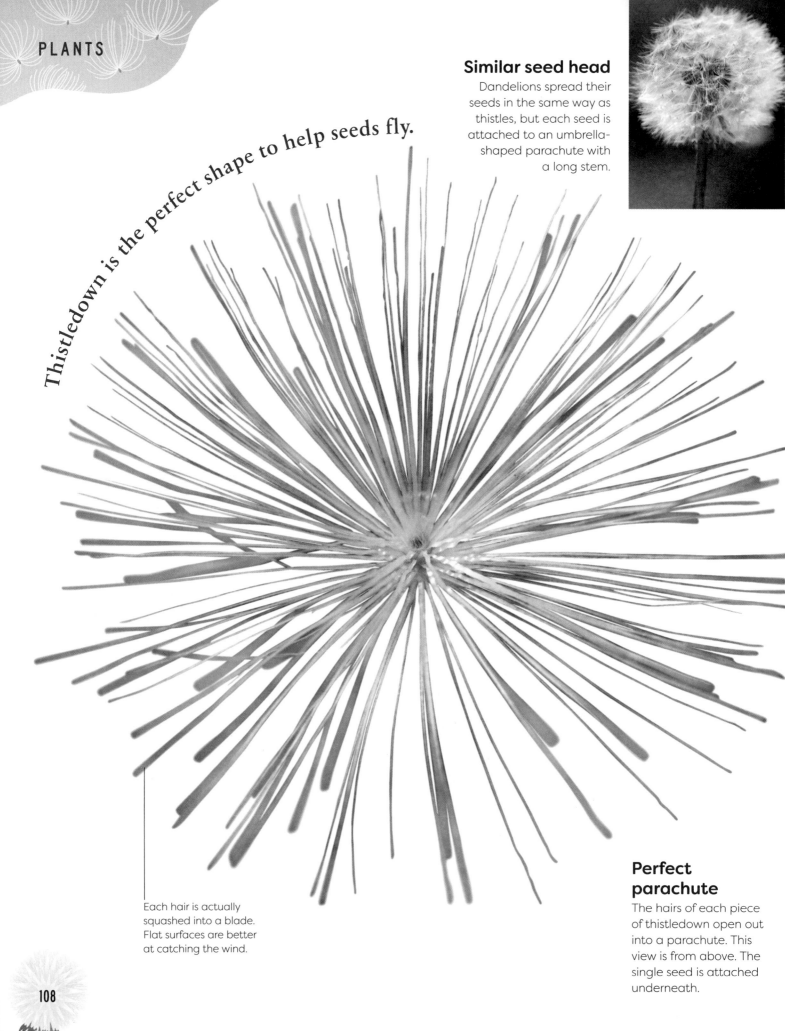

Thistledown is the perfect shape to help seeds fly.

Similar seed head

Dandelions spread their seeds in the same way as thistles, but each seed is attached to an umbrella-shaped parachute with a long stem.

Each hair is actually squashed into a blade. Flat surfaces are better at catching the wind.

Perfect parachute

The hairs of each piece of thistledown open out into a parachute. This view is from above. The single seed is attached underneath.

Thistledown

Fluffy thistledown transports seeds far and wide, wherever the wind takes it.

Thistles are tall and elegant plants with tufted purple, red, or pink flowers. All summer, their plentiful nectar attracts masses of insects. This makes them a valuable part of grassland habitats and a great addition to wildlife gardens. Thistles have a long flowering season, but, eventually, they wilt and dry out. Their flowers then turn into thistledown, clumps of which look like the fluffy tails of rabbits.

For a while, not much else happens. Then, a gentle breeze picks up, and the balls of fluff start to fall apart. Individual stars of the pale fuzz float up and away across the sky—hundreds of them, like a snowstorm, but in summer. Every piece of thistledown is carrying a precious cargo, a thistle seed. Many seeds will be blown to unwelcoming places, such as water, sand, or pavement. These seeds are doomed. However, seeds that land in soil have a chance of sprouting the following spring. By riding the wind, thistles can spread rapidly. Thistles can also spread by networks of roots that creep through the soil. There is no stopping them!

Purple star thistle
(Centaurea calcitrapa)
This common thistle grows in grassy places around the world. On farmland, it is often seen as a weed.

Seed

Seed head

Carried on the breeze

In late summer, thistle flowers ripen into cream-colored seed heads. They are loosely packed with seeds, each of which has a tuft of fine hairs. The wind tugs these tufts off the seed heads, taking the lightweight seeds with them.

Horse chestnut tree
(Aesculus hippocastanum)
This tree's original home is in the mountains of southeastern Europe, but it has been planted worldwide in gardens and city parks.

Chestnut

Horse chestnut trees scatter these shiny seeds by using the force of gravity.

If you walk under horse chestnut trees in fall, beware. Falling chestnuts might thump you on the head. Chestnuts are heavy seeds squeezed into prickly cases, which are, in fact, fruit. When the fruit drop to the ground with a clunk, the impact cracks them open and their hidden treasure is revealed. The chestnuts are smooth, glossy, and a handsome red-brown color.

Two centuries ago, children in Great Britain and Ireland began collecting chestnuts every fall for a fun game they had invented. The first record of it being played was in 1848, and it was called conkers. To play, a hole was made in the chosen chestnut so a piece of string could be attached. The children took turns swinging the chestnut at their opponent's chestnut, or conker. The player who smashed their rival's chestnut to bits won. If you ever want to try this game yourself, take care not to hit anyone (or yourself) with the conker. Never be tempted to taste a chestnut, because these seeds are bitter and slightly poisonous to humans. Squirrels, wild boar, and deer love them, though. Sometimes squirrels bury the chestnuts as a food supply, but before they can eat them, the seeds grow into new trees.

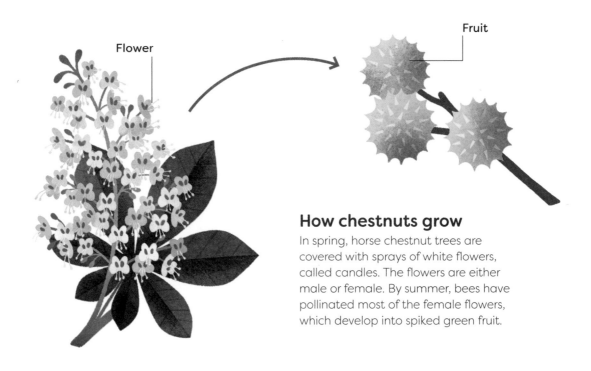

Flower

Fruit

How chestnuts grow
In spring, horse chestnut trees are covered with sprays of white flowers, called candles. The flowers are either male or female. By summer, bees have pollinated most of the female flowers, which develop into spiked green fruit.

Round seed

Each case protects a tough, plump seed—the chestnut. The pale circle on one side is where the chestnut was attached to its case.

The spikes on a horse chestnut fruit are strong and sharp.

When the fruit splits open, it reveals the chestnut, or chestnuts, inside.

Over time, a chestnut case changes from green to yellow.

Spiked case

The spiked husk around a chestnut is bright green and leathery outside, with soft white padding inside.

Seeds

Seeds are beautifully wrapped packages from which new plants grow. A seed's hard case contains a baby plant, or embryo, and food supplies to get it started. Seeds may sprout immediately, or wait in the soil. Scientists once grew a tree from a 2,000-year-old seed!

Traveler's palm

This unusual seed, from a tree from Madagascar, has a blue case that attracts lemurs. Blue seeds are rare in nature because the color does not appeal to most animals.

Avocado

Each avocado fruit has a single huge seed, called a pit. The seeds were once eaten and spread by mammoths—giant, hairy elephants that became extinct long ago.

Common poppy

Poppy seeds are tiny (this one is shown hugely magnified) and are held inside a fragile seed head. Wind rattles the seed head like a maraca and the seeds are sprinkled out.

Lotus

Lotus plants are from Asia and look a bit like water lilies. After flowering, they produce plump seeds that drop into the water of ponds and lakes so new plants can grow.

Ginkgo

China's ginkgo tree is so ancient it comes from a time before flowers and fruits existed. It produces white seeds inside what looks like a round yellow fruit, which can smell awful.

Exploding cucumber

These seeds are poisonous and ripen in a pod, like beans and peas. When the seeds are ripe, the pod squirts out a jet of gooey liquid, throwing the seeds a few feet or more.

How seeds spread

Seeds are adapted to travel away from the parent plant in different ways. Some get eaten by animals or stick to their fur. Others use gravity, the wind, or flowing water to be transported. Some even explode out as their seed case heats up or dries out.

Falling

Animals

Water

Wind

Explosion

The brown husk protects the seed inside.

Rice

Rice is grown widely for its seeds, which are eaten as a grain. Often the outer brown husk of each rice seed is removed to produce white rice.

Runner bean

The beans we eat are actually seeds, which form inside dangly pods. If left on the plant, the pods dry out and burst open, scattering the beans over the soil.

Some varieties of runner beans have colorful patterns.

Sprouting seed

A big coconut weighs around 3 lb (1.5 kg),
yet it easily floats across the sea to reach new beaches.
If swept ashore, the smooth fruit sprouts a stem and
roots from the single seed inside. The sand lacks
nutrients, but the seedling is sustained by the flesh
and watery "milk" inside the seed.

Piling up

Huge heaps of saltwort tumbleweed are blown against fences and buildings. Because they are bone-dry, they can be a fire risk.

A tangle of twisted branches and dry leaves makes a ball shape.

The tumbleweed snaps off from its roots at the base of its stem.

Seed spreader

Saltwort produces enormous quantities of seeds. These don't need much water to sprout, so the plant spreads rapidly, wherever it rolls.

A single tumbleweed can contain up to 200,000 seeds.

Tumbleweed

Prickly balls of tumbleweed roll across the land, spreading their seeds as they go.

There is not one species of tumbleweed but many. They are mainly found in wide, dusty plains, such as those in the American prairies, Russia's vast grasslands, and the Australian outback. The thing that all these plants have in common is an extraordinary way of spreading their seeds. Up until the moment they flower, they look fairly ordinary, but then the transformation begins. Entire plants dry out in the sun and harden, so that they become no more than brittle balls full of seeds. Then their stem snaps and they are off. All they need is a windy day.

In December 2020, fierce storms in the Midwestern United States brought an invasion of tumbleweeds. Strong winds sent the tumbleweeds bouncing into towns and across highways, where they buried cars and even a huge tractor trailer. In the fall of 1989, in the state of South Dakota whole houses were swamped in tumbleweeds, and the owners had to be dug out. It is fair to say that few plants cause so much chaos.

Common saltwort
(Kali tragus)
Saltwort is a tough plant that thrives in salty earth, especially in the central US. It is famous for forming large tumbleweeds.

Seeds

Tumbling in the wind
After saltwort has flowered, its leaves shrivel up and its branches curl into a ball. The dead plant breaks away from its roots and gusts of wind can now roll the ball over the ground. It scatters seeds as it goes, like a pepper shaker scattering pepper.

117

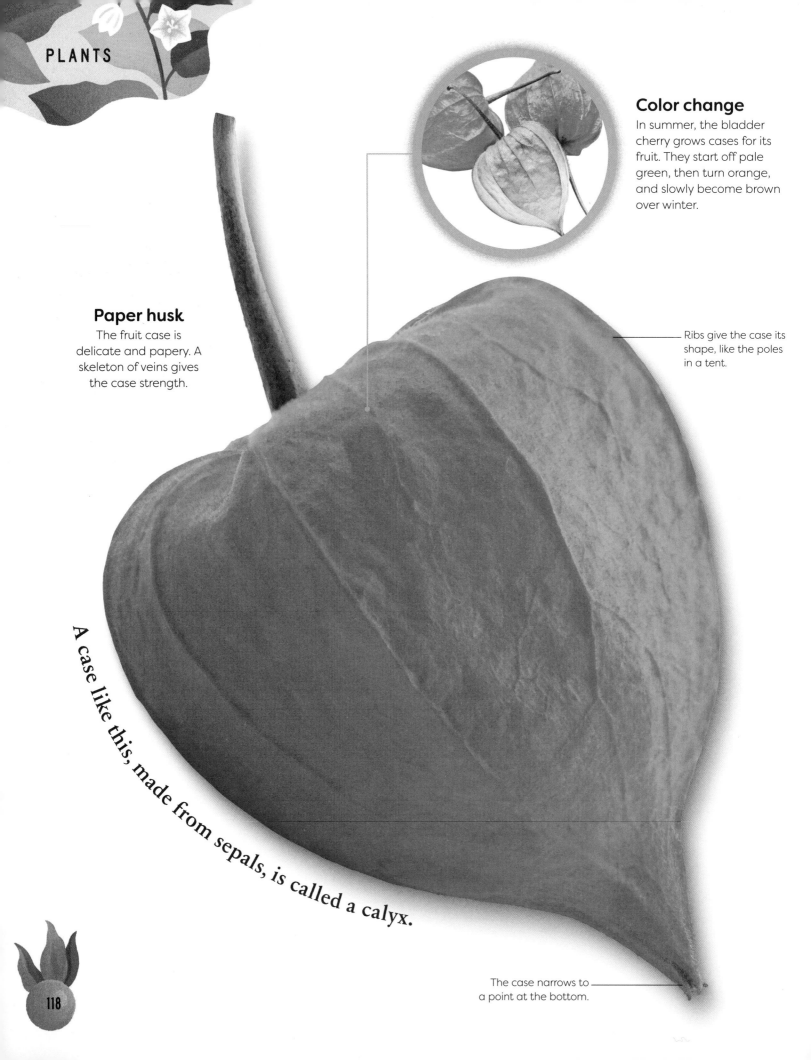

Color change

In summer, the bladder cherry grows cases for its fruit. They start off pale green, then turn orange, and slowly become brown over winter.

Ribs give the case its shape, like the poles in a tent.

Paper husk

The fruit case is delicate and papery. A skeleton of veins gives the case strength.

A case like this, made from sepals, is called a calyx.

The case narrows to a point at the bottom.

118

Paper lantern case

The bladder cherry covers its fruit in a colorful wrapper like a paper lantern.

Gardeners love this plant, so you can spot a bladder cherry in many flowerbeds and pots across the globe. It is not grown for its leaves or flowers, though. There are many other plants to choose from with more spectacular foliage and blooms. People grow bladder cherries for the unusual orange pods they produce at the end of the summer. These look a little like seed heads, but are not. They develop from the sepals, the green and leaflike outer parts of the plant's flower, and protect the fruit inside.

The fruit cases get their name from their resemblance to paper lanterns, which are paper cyclinders that glow when a small candle in the middle is lit. They are popular worldwide, particularly in Asia. Real paper lanterns must be used with care because they can cause litter and start fires. The plant lanterns, however, are used at several Buddhist festivals. In Japan, they are gathered and hung up for Obon, the Festival of the Dead. People in Japan celebrate Obon every year to guide the spirits of their ancestors home.

Bladder cherry
(Physalis alkekengi)
This plant from Asia and Europe is a member of the tomato family. It has many similar relatives in Central and South America.

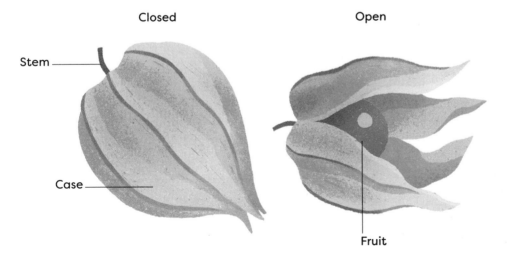

Closed

Open

Stem

Case

Fruit

Open case
During winter, the fruit cases weaken and split open. Tucked inside is a bright fruit that looks like a tiny orange tomato. It is only edible when ripe and contains more vitamin C than citrus fruit. Beware: other parts of the plant are very poisonous!

Pieces of the veil remain on the cap as white spots.

The veil protected the stem as it grew taller.

Frilly gills
These thin flaps under the cap are where the spores are stored. When the gills dry out, the spores will be released.

Toadstools live for just a few days.

Warning colors
The red cap is a bright warning to animals that if they eat this toadstool they will soon start to feel very sick, or worse. Better to find some other food!

The toadstool sprouts from a network of very fine underground threads.

Toadstool

This umbrella-shaped toadstool has bright colors as a warning. It is poisonous, so just look and don't touch.

This red-capped toadstool sticks out of the ground on a tall stem, but it is not a plant. It is part of a fungus called the fly agaric. Fungi are life-forms separate from animals and plants. Most of the time we would not know they are even there—they usually grow in the soil as wispy threads called hyphae. Usually, fungi feed on the remains of other living organisms—anything from wood to dung! To eat, they spread all over and inside their food and give out digestive juices that break it up. Then the fungi simply absorb the nutrients they need. Eventually, there is nothing left. In this way, fungi help to rot away the remains of other organisms.

But what is a toadstool for? When certain fungi want to spread to new areas, they sprout a toadstool, or mushroom. The cap of the toadstool is filled with tiny spores, which are like minute seeds. These are blown away by the wind far and wide. Some mushrooms can be eaten, but many more are deadly poisonous. Never touch or taste mushrooms or toadstools growing in the wild.

Fly agaric
(*Amanita muscaria*)
This fungus lives all over northern areas of the world. It is most common in forests of pine and birch trees.

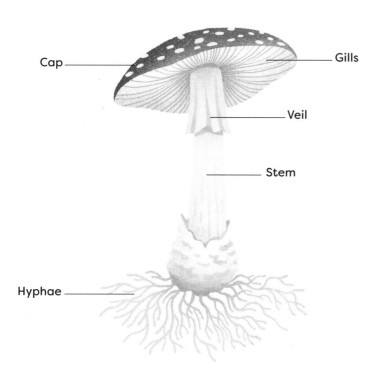

Cap ——— Gills

——— Veil

——— Stem

Hyphae ———

Mushroom or toadstool?

All mushrooms and toadstools are built in the same kind of way, and there is no scientific difference between them. Fungi sprout in a huge variety of shapes and colors, and many have unusual names, such as powdery piggyback, stinkhorn, and jelly ear.

Over half of the planet's oxygen is made by marine algae, including seaweed.

Fronds are tough and leathery to cope with rough waves.

The air bubbles are found in twos, on each side of the central rib.

A central rib makes the frond sturdier.

Leaf or frond?

Each branch of bladder wrack flattens out into wavy straps, which are called fronds. These certainly look leafy but are not really leaves.

Bladder wrack

This seaweed contains a clever system of air bubbles to help it rise and fall with the tides.

Seaweeds are submerged in the ocean much of the time, so to get a good look at bladder wrack, you have to wait until the tide goes out. On a rocky coast, there will often be mounds of it along the shoreline. It feels slimy and smells of the salty sea. What is it, though? A plant, or something else? Most biologists now agree that brown seaweeds, such as bladder wrack, are not plants, but kinds of algae. This is because they don't have proper roots, stems, or leaves, and they reproduce in a different way. Instead of roots, seaweeds have an anchor, called a holdfast, which grips the seabed, and instead of leaves, they have simple ribbonlike fronds.

Bladder wrack has distinctive fronds that are studded with little balloons. These bubbles of air help the fronds to stay upright in the water, so they reach toward the sun. Seaweeds absorb some nutrients straight from seawater, but they also make food from sunlight by photosynthesis. While plants use green pigments to do this, bladder wrack pigments are brown. These work better in the murky light—and give bladder wrack its color.

Bladder wrack
(Fucus vesiculosus)
Every seaweed has its favorite spot. This one grows in the middle of the shore, on the northern coasts of the Atlantic and Pacific oceans.

High and low
At high tide, seawater covers the bladder wrack. Its gas-filled air bubbles float and pull its fronds upright, so they receive plenty of sunlight. At low tide, the bladder wrack collapses into a wet heap.

Low tide

High tide

123

CHAPTER 3

Minerals

and rocks

Minerals are building blocks of
the Earth. They form the rocks that
shape the surface of the planet, from its
ocean floor to its continents. They shape
the human world, too, by providing us
with construction materials, fuel, and
dazzling gemstones. Rocks and minerals
can even tell us what life was like
millions of years ago!

This diamond has been cut into a pear shape, with one pointed end.

Colorless diamonds are the ones most often used in jewelry.

Colorful crystals

Some diamonds don't have any color, but most have faint tints. Brown or yellow diamonds are the most common, while pink, blue, green, and red are rarer.

On Uranus and Neptune, it probably rains diamonds!

Many sides

Jewelers cut many flat surfaces, or facets, into a diamond. This produces a sparkly rainbow effect called fire, as light bounces through the gemstone.

Diamond

Diamonds are one of the hardest and most long-lasting natural objects.

It is almost impossible to destroy a diamond. These tough crystals of carbon get 10 out of 10 on the hardness scale for minerals. The name diamond actually comes from an ancient Greek word that means indestructible. Being so tough, sharpened diamonds are used in powerful drills to cut metal and stone. We also give diamond rings as a sign of everlasting love. Surprisingly, diamonds are made from the same stuff as the lead in pencils. Pencil lead is graphite, and graphite, like diamonds, is 100 percent carbon. Their amazing differences are due to how their building blocks of carbon are put together.

In 1869, the discovery of a huge diamond in South Africa started a diamond rush. Many mines opened and the gem's popularity took off, but mining diamonds can be difficult work. It is now possible to make artificial diamonds in a laboratory, by copying the natural conditions in which they form. Diamonds are not naturally bright and glittering. To make them shine, jewelers cut them into all sorts of shapes. There are not many things that can cut a diamond though—sometimes other diamonds are used.

Kimberlite

Today, we get most of our diamonds from inside a dark volcanic rock called kimberlite. It is named after the town of Kimberley in South Africa.

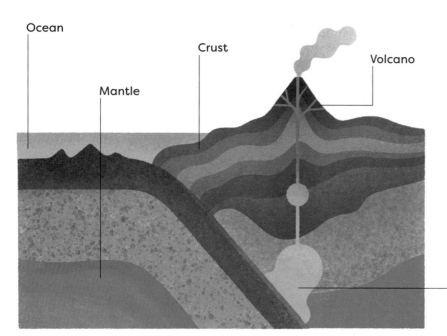

Ocean

Mantle

Crust

Volcano

Magma

How diamonds are made

It takes immense heat and pressure to turn carbon into diamonds. You find these conditions deep underground, in liquid rock about 90 miles (150 km) below our feet. Three or four billion years ago, this rock was forced to the surface by volcanic eruptions, taking the diamonds with it.

Gems

People throughout history have been in awe of gemstones, or gems. These minerals get their stunning colors from the materials they contain. Many are cut or polished to make them shine or sparkle. Gems are rare, which is why we value them as jewels.

Turquoise

This gem is bluish-green because it contains copper and iron. It also often has dark veins of rust running through it. The ancient Egyptians crafted necklaces and charms from turquoise.

Sapphire

Most sapphires are deep blue, but they can be green or yellow, too. Whatever the color, they are made from a hard mineral called corundum, which is the material that also makes rubies.

Ruby

Rubies are closely related to sapphires. Both are made from the mineral corundum and are often found in gravel. However, unlike sapphires, rubies are blood-red or pink.

Carnelian

People from the Mediterranean have valued this orangey-red gem for 10,000 years. It was often used as an official seal—it was carved with an image, then dipped in hot wax to stamp documents.

Jade

Pure jade is white, but iron turns it green. The more iron, the greener it is. In ancient central America, green jade was thought to have great power. It was carved into masks used in religious rituals.

Opal

Opals develop when water drips into cracks in sandstone. They come in many colors, but are often green and blue. They flash different colors like disco lights as you turn them around.

Emerald

These gems are deep green and very rare. You might be surprised to learn that diamonds are far more common! Emeralds are made of a mineral called beryl, which in its pure form has no color at all.

An emerald cut as an octagon has eight sides when seen from above.

Moonstone

This gem doesn't come from the moon—it gets its name for how it shimmers, like moonlight on water. Some people believe moonstone has healing properties and brings good luck.

Moonstone's delicate surface varies from milky white to the palest blue.

Gem cuts

Gems are cut and polished to bring out their beauty. Expert craftspeople work the rough stone with great patience and skill. They shape the stone and create many different angles until it dazzles.

Round

Pear

Oval

Square

Emerald

Octagon

129

Geode

Some rocks look ordinary, until you split
them open to reveal a hidden world of sparkly crystals.
The crystals form when a hole in a rock fills with
mineral-rich liquid and a geode is created. In this
example, the rock contains the gemstone agate,
which is filled with swirling galaxies of color.

Out of 100 snowflakes, only one will grow to be perfectly symmetrical.

Snowflake symmetry

A perfect snowflake has six points and six lines of symmetry. This means there are six ways to cut it in half.

Branches and side-branches create a feathery pattern.

Ice is clear, so light passes through it.

Fractal patterns

If you look closely at a snowflake, you will see its branching pattern. If you look even closer, you will see that the pattern repeats itself on a smaller scale. Patterns like these are called fractals.

Snowflake

When water in the air freezes, it creates twinkling ice crystals that float to the ground.

If the air is cold enough, droplets of water freeze into tiny crystals of ice high in the sky, often in clouds. These are the beginnings of snowflakes. As more water freezes onto the crystals, they start to grow. Billions of the heavy snowflakes now whirl downward, still growing and changing shape as they fall. This is a snowstorm, one of the great sights of nature. So long as the ground is at or below 32°F (0°C), the snow will pile up. Soon, everything is white... or is it? Snowflakes appear white, both in the air and on the ground, but they are actually colorless. The whiteness comes from their complex shape, which bounces light in all directions.

It is hard to appreciate the beauty of individual snowflakes because they are so fragile and clump together, hiding their real shape. One way to do it is to photograph them in close-up using a super-cold microscope—then their beautiful six-sided symmetry is revealed. However, most snowflakes are uneven or lopsided because parts of them melt as they fall through the air.

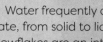

Water
Water frequently changes state, from solid to liquid or gas. Snowflakes are an intricate form of solid ice crystals.

Never the same
All snowflakes are unique. This is because they all take different paths to the ground, passing through air at different temperatures and with different amounts of moisture. There is no limit to the number of shapes that snowflakes can form.

133

Amber

Honey-colored amber is a special type of fossil that can preserve extinct species.

Unlike stone, which is cold to the touch, amber feels nice and warm. It is also much lighter and softer than stone, and it may contain air bubbles that help it float. Most amber is see-through, like golden glass. No wonder this mysterious material has always fascinated us. Ever since the Stone Age, it has been carved into jewelry and ornaments. The ancient Greeks believed amber was solid drops of sunlight, while other people thought it was the tears of birds or gods.

The truth is that amber is the fossilized remains of a natural resin. This syrupy liquid is produced by conifer trees to heal damaged bark. It oozes out in gloopy globs, which harden to seal any wounds. Sometimes, unfortunate insects land in the sticky substance and are trapped in it. When chunks of the hard resin fall to the ground and are buried, they—and any animals trapped inside—may slowly turn into fossils. You can find amber in many parts of the world. Often it is washed by rivers into the sea and ends up on beaches, bashed and scratched by the waves and sand.

Conifer tree
(Pinophyta)

Most amber comes from conifers that first grew in huge forests millions of years ago, when the climate was warmer.

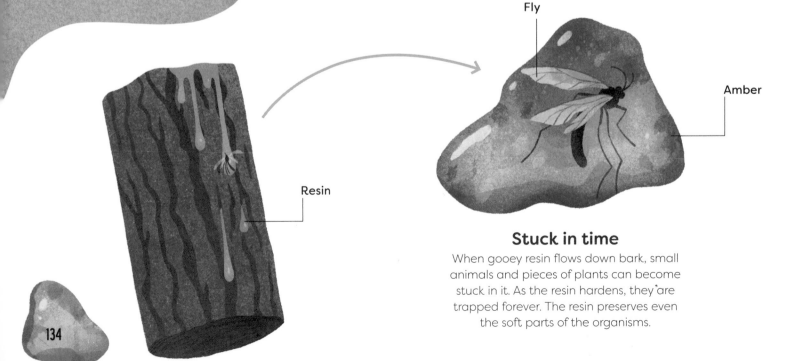

Fly

Amber

Resin

Stuck in time

When gooey resin flows down bark, small animals and pieces of plants can become stuck in it. As the resin hardens, they are trapped forever. The resin preserves even the soft parts of the organisms.

Time capsule
All kinds of things have been preserved in amber in the past. These include seeds, pollen, flies, ants, beetles, caterpillars, spiders, and even the feathers and skulls of tiny dinosaurs.

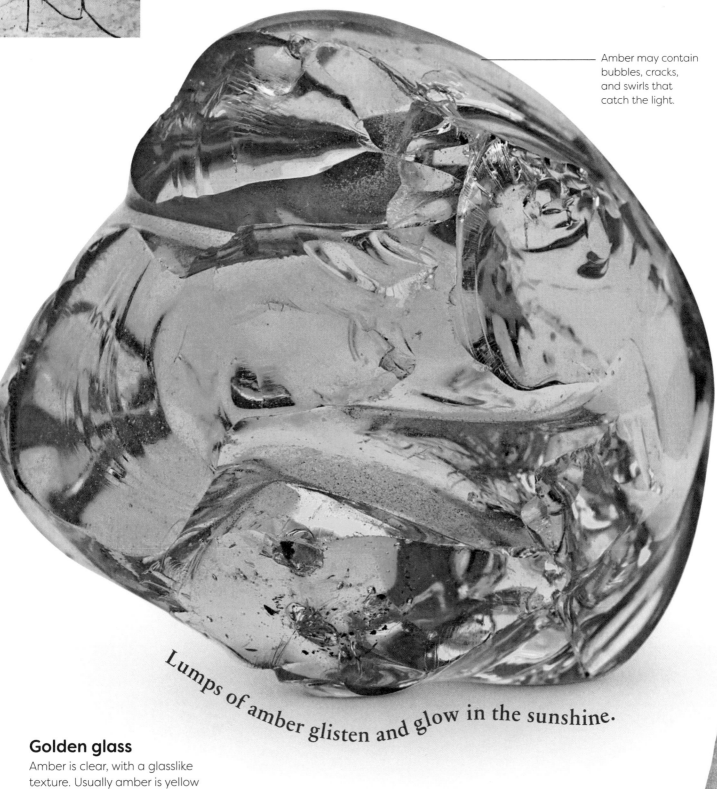

Amber may contain bubbles, cracks, and swirls that catch the light.

Lumps of amber glisten and glow in the sunshine.

Golden glass
Amber is clear, with a glasslike texture. Usually amber is yellow or orange, but rare varieties can look green or blue in the sun.

Gleam and shine

Pearls have a gentle gleam, unlike the dramatic sparkle of diamonds and other mineral gems.

Oysters start life as males, but turn into females after a few years.

A piece of sand or grit lies in the center of the pearl.

The pearl's surface is as hard and smooth as a billiard ball.

Rare color

Most pearls are white. Very occasionally, black-lip pearl oysters produce black pearls, but only one in 10,000 have this darker color.

Oyster pearl

Pearls are shiny gemstones that grow inside oyster shells.

Few things are more annoying than dirt in your eye or a tiny pebble in your shoe. Oysters, which live on the seabed, also become irritated when a piece of grit or sand gets into their shell. Usually this happens when their hinged shell is open to feed. To prevent any damage to their soft bodies, the oysters cover the grit or sand with a material called mother-of-pearl, or nacre. This is the shiny substance that lines the inside of their shell, and it is incredibly hard and strong. Like body armor, the reinforced shell protects the oysters against crabs and other predators that try to smash their way in.

Mussels also form pearls, but all natural pearls are rare. Today, most oyster pearls are farmed. The oyster farmer opens each shell ever so carefully, then places a bead inside. This starts the development of an artificial pearl. Not all pearls are round balls—some stay stuck to the inside of the shell's surface and form odd shapes. Not all pearls are white either—different minerals in the nacre can make pearls in a rainbow of colors.

Black-lip pearl oyster
(Pinctada margaritifera)
Many pearls are gathered from black-lip pearl oysters, which live on coral reefs in the Indian and Pacific oceans.

Making a pearl

If a grain of sand is sucked into an oyster's shell, it can stick fast to the inside. The oyster surrounds the sand in layers of nacre that build up over time. Small pearls grow in under a year, while larger ones take several years.

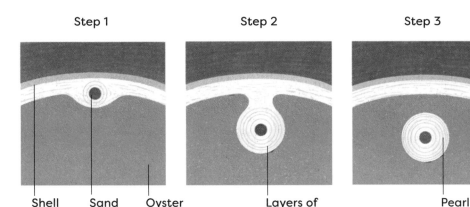

Step 1 — Shell   Sand   Oyster

Step 2 — Layers of nacre

Step 3 — Pearl detaches

Pyrite

The dazzling mineral pyrite can look like it was created by a machine.

In the past, many a treasure hunter was fooled by this golden substance. When they saw it, they thought they had gotten lucky and struck gold. Only later did they realize their mistake. What they had actually found was not the valuable metal they were looking for, but pyrite—a common mineral whose yellow color comes from sulfur. This is why pyrite is also known as "fool's gold." In fact, there is a simple way to tell pyrite and gold apart. The surface is scraped with an iron nail. Real gold is a soft metal, so a nail will make an obvious scratch in the nugget. However, on tougher pyrite, a nail will not leave any visible mark.

Although this shiny mineral is worthless compared to gold, it has still played a big part in human history. If it is hit hard with a rock or blade, it gives off a shower of sparks. For thousands of years, this is how people started fires. Pyrite helped them to light up the dark, keep warm, cook food, and frighten away dangerous animals.

Pyrite

This abundant mineral is found worldwide. It is made from a combination of iron and sulfur.

Cube crystals

There are several kinds of pyrite, each with different shapes of crystal. In the most common variety, the crystals are all smooth-sided cubes. Perfect cubes like these are rare in the natural world.

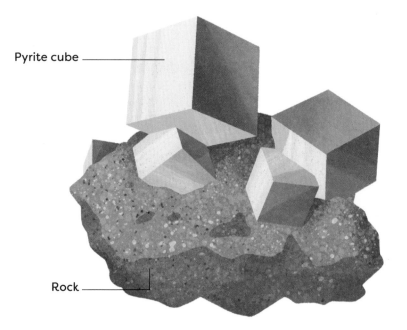

Pyrite cube

Rock

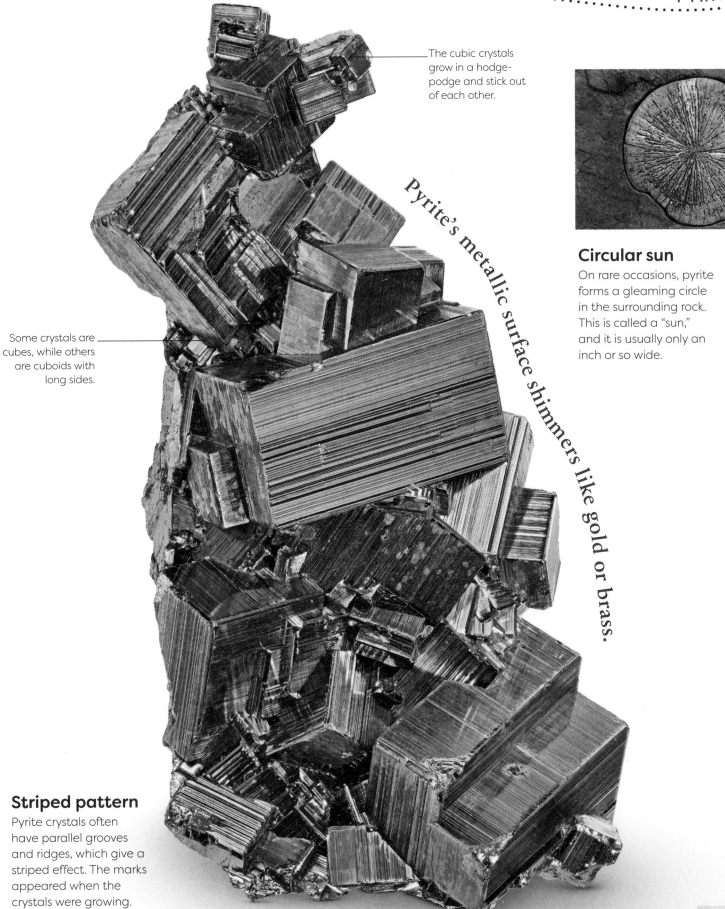

The cubic crystals grow in a hodge-podge and stick out of each other.

Some crystals are cubes, while others are cuboids with long sides.

Pyrite's metallic surface shimmers like gold or brass.

Circular sun

On rare occasions, pyrite forms a gleaming circle in the surrounding rock. This is called a "sun," and it is usually only an inch or so wide.

Striped pattern

Pyrite crystals often have parallel grooves and ridges, which give a striped effect. The marks appeared when the crystals were growing.

Malachite often has bands of light and dark green.

Malachite

This bright green mineral is an ore of copper. It is often found in round lumps. Malachite can be used to make copper, but this colorful mineral is also used in jewelry and carvings.

The red speckles on the hematite's surface are spots of rust.

Hematite

Hematite is a shiny gray mineral. It is one of the most important ores of iron. There is so much iron in the ore that it can conduct electricity.

Element or mineral?

An element is the simplest kind of substance that can't be split up into any more ingredients. Gold and many other metals are elements. A mineral, like malachite, is different. Minerals are made up of two or more elements and usually grow in crystals.

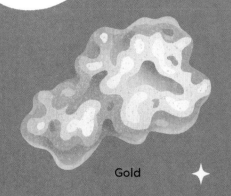

Gold

Malachite

Metal ores

An ore is a rock or mineral that contains a useful substance—very often a metal such as copper or iron. Miners search hard for these ores, looking for large clumps, or seams, underground. The lovely colors and shapes of the ores help show which metals are locked away inside.

Sphalerite

This glittering mineral is an ore of zinc, a soft, silvery metal. Its crystals have many flat sides that are almost as shiny as a mirror. In addition to zinc, the ore contains iron and sulfur.

Scheelite

These orange crystals are a complicated mineral made up of the metals calcium and tungsten, along with oxygen. Scheelite is used to make pure tungsten, which is used in light bulbs.

Galena

This heavy, shiny ore looks and feels like pure metal. In fact, it is a mix of lead and sulfur. In addition to being used to make lead—which is found in car batteries—galena is also sometimes a source of silver.

Bauxite

This rock is an important ore of the metal aluminum. Aluminum is very common, but it is hard to make it pure. Bauxite has to be melted and electrified to get the metal out of it.

Acanthite

Dark and soft, this strange mineral is full of silver. Its name comes from the ancient Greek word for "arrow," because its crystals are pointed, with spikes. This ore is often found in cracks between other rocks.

Cassiterite

These beautiful dark crystals are an ore of tin. Cassiterite is one of the oldest ores to be used. In ancient civilizations, tin was mixed with copper to make tough bronze, used in statues and swords.

Fossil fuel

Because coal originally came from ancient plants and it burns well, we call it a fossil fuel. When set alight, it reacts with oxygen in the air and gives off intense heat.

Two textures

Pieces of coal are rough in some places and smooth in others. They leave behind a shadow of fine black dust when moved.

Coal is brittle and cracks easily.

Some parts of the coal's surface are shiny while others are dull.

Coal has powered the human world for hundreds of years.

Coal

Coal is a dark rock that formed from the squashed remains of ancient plants.

More than 300 million years ago, when the planet was warm and wet, massive swamps covered the land. There were huge ferns and strange treelike plants taller than a 10-story building. Giant insects buzzed through the tropical air. There were not yet any really large animals and definitely no dinosaurs—they arrived much later. This mysterious time is known as the Carboniferous Period. Plants from this period, which became fossilized and turned to rock, are the source of coal.

Lumps of coal are full of energy and they can be burned to produce roaring fires. However, coal lies underground between layers of other types of rock, so it can only be reached by digging mines. In the 1700s, people began mining large amounts of coal to fuel factories, run machines, and heat homes, and later it was used to generate electricity in power plants. It is amazing to think that this simple rock gave birth to modern industry. Coal can be harmful, though. Burning coal pollutes the air and releases carbon dioxide gas, which contributes to climate change.

Scale tree
(Lepidodendron)
The remains of different types of plant survive as coal. One important source was scale trees. These enormous treelike organisms were some of the first tall plants on Earth.

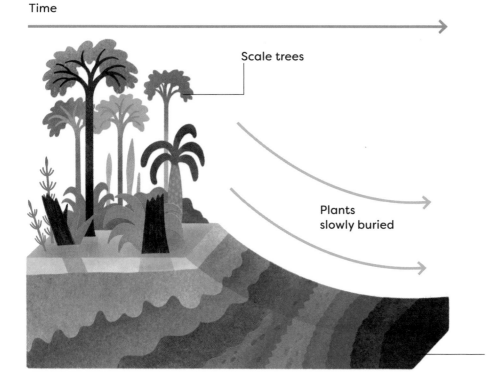

Time

Scale trees

Plants
slowly buried

Coal

Coal formation
During the Carboniferous Period, in tropical swamps, plants died and rotted in the wet ground. More rotting plants then fell on top. Sediment and soil were buried with the plant remains, and over millions of years, they were pressed into coal.

143

Most seashells are made from the same material as chalk.

Lots of layers

Chalk is found under the ground. Most chalk formed about 80 million years ago and today it can be seen in thick white bands alongside other layers of rock.

Chalk is all one color, with no obvious mineral crystals inside it.

Crumbly rock

Chalk is a bright gray-white color. It feels soft and almost greasy as its tiny fragments crumble under your fingertips.

Solid chalk is filled with tiny holes, which soak up water.

Chalk

This soft, crumbly rock is made from the skeletons and shells of tiny sea creatures.

Chalk is a familiar white rock with a surprising past. It formed deep beneath the seabed many millions of years ago and much later was pushed back up to the surface for us to see and touch. However, it is not its age that is unusual but where it came from. The main ingredient of chalk is the mineral calcium carbonate, which is made in many ways in nature. For example, it is the mineral found inside the hard shells of animals such as clams and snails. It also makes the skeletons of certain miniature ocean life-forms. They are far too small to see without a microscope, but when they die and sink to the bottom of the ocean, their piled-up skeletons can become squashed into chalk!

Chalk is soft stuff, and it leaves a streak of white when scraped against a harder surface. Once, people used natural chalk for writing and drawing, but today's writing chalks are made from other materials. Chalk is also used to make the cement that holds brick walls together, and it is added to soil to help certain plants grow.

Chalk
Some of the best places to see chalk are cliffs along the seaside, especially in England and France.

Chalk creator
The tiny organisms that make chalk are types of algae. This alga, called a coccolithophore, has a hard outer skeleton made from disk-shaped plates of calcium carbonate. These life-forms were much more common when the dinosaurs were alive, and their remains created the chalk we see today.

Skeleton is made of overlapping plates

145

Flint

This dark and glassy stone was used in the Stone Age for cutting and slicing.

Flint is often found in disguise. It looks like a rounded stone with smooth sides and a pale yellowish color. However, once the rock is smashed open, the flint reveals its dark and shiny insides. This rock is made from the mineral quartz, which is a natural mineral made from silicon and oxygen. Quartz is very common stuff—most of the world's sand is made from little see-through quartz crystals— and it comes in a variety of colors and crystal shapes. The quartz in flint looks very different, though. There are no crystals to be seen inside the stone. Instead, the mineral is dark, smooth, and shiny—a bit like a piece of glass. Just like glass, when flint breaks, its pieces always have very sharp, curved edges.

Early humans, going back at least 3 million years, learnt to break up lumps of flint to make stone axes and other blades useful for cutting up food. We call this period of time the Stone Age, because our ancient ancestors made tools from rocks, rather than metals.

Flint

Flint is made when blobs of quartz get trapped inside limestone and chalk. Here they are squashed into the hard, round stone over millions of years.

Knapping an arrow

Flint arrowheads are created by a process known as knapping. To knap, a craftsperson uses another stone to carefully chip away small flakes of flint to create a sharp, pointed shape. Knapping is quite a skill. One wrong move and the whole arrowhead could crack in two!

Blunt point

Sharp point

Is it flint?

Flint can range from black through to dark and light gray and brown. However, it isn't see-through like volcanic glass.

The broken edges inside flint are wavy, not straight.

A coating of powdery paler flint covers the rock inside.

Flint was once used to make arrows, axes, and scrapers.

Magical stone?

Some pieces of flint have natural holes in them. According to legend, the hole is a gateway to a hidden fairy kingdom.

When flint breaks, it forms sharp points.

Where the rock gets thinner, it is more see-through, like glass.

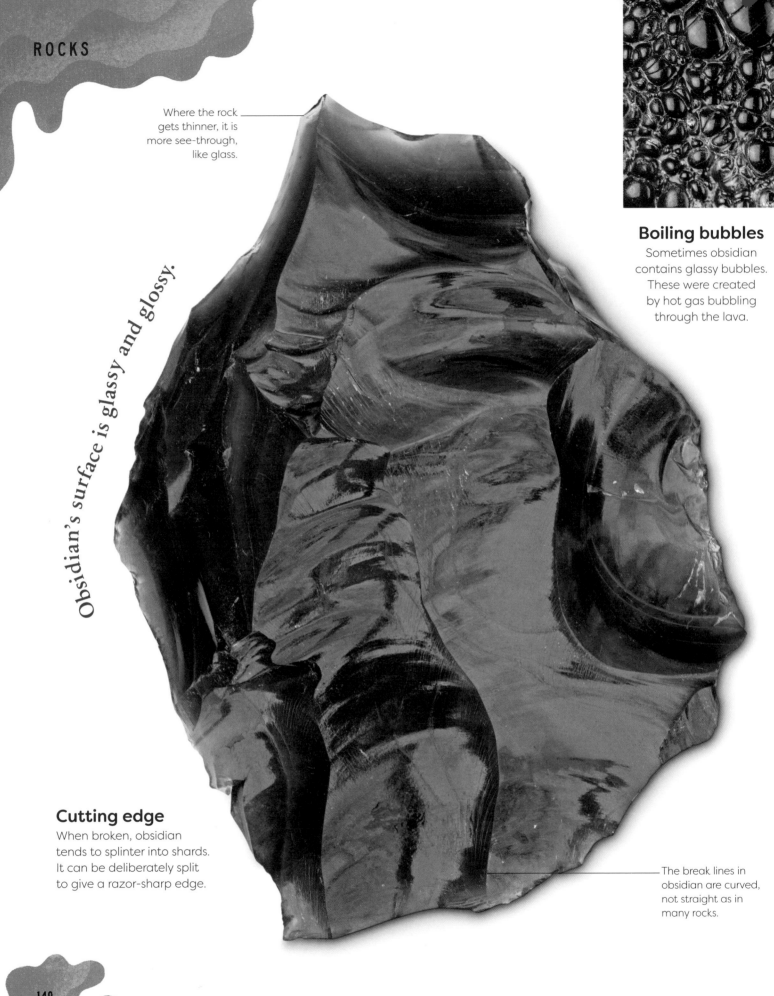

Boiling bubbles
Sometimes obsidian contains glassy bubbles. These were created by hot gas bubbling through the lava.

Obsidian's surface is glassy and glossy.

Cutting edge
When broken, obsidian tends to splinter into shards. It can be deliberately split to give a razor-sharp edge.

The break lines in obsidian are curved, not straight as in many rocks.

Obsidian

This marvel of nature is as black as the night sky and the smoothest rock there is.

Volcanic eruptions are violent and terrifying, but they don't just cause immense destruction. They can also shape new landscapes, create fertile soil with their ash, and give birth to beautiful rocks. One of these is obsidian, which forms only in certain special conditions. It is created when lava cools rapidly, but only from volcanoes found on land, never underwater. It is a rock unlike any other rock. In fact, it looks more like glass and obsidian is often called volcanic glass.

Like glass, obsidian shatters easily to produce a cutting edge. Early humans realized this and used the sharp material to make knives and arrowheads. Its great advantage was that the blades stayed sharp for a long time. Later, many peoples around the world cut obsidian for jewelry and other decorative items. In ancient Egypt, pieces of obsidian were used to make the shiny black eyes of King Tutankhamun's death mask. The Aztec people of Mexico associated obsidian with the gods. They polished it into shiny black mirrors, which they believed were magical and could see into other worlds.

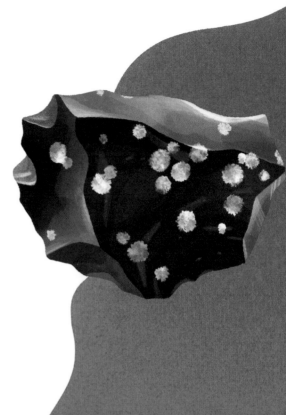

Snowflake obsidian
You find obsidian on land, wherever there are volcanoes. Sometimes it contains white spots, which are called "snowflakes." These are made of the mineral cristobalite.

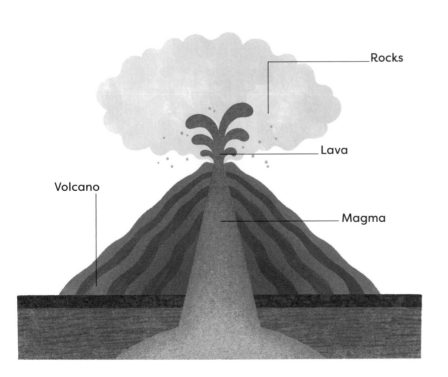

Rocks

Lava

Volcano

Magma

Fiery beginning
The sticky lava that streams out of a volcano can reach 2,200 °F (1,200 °C). If it cools rapidly and hardens, there is no time for crystals to grow in it. Then it transforms into the substance we call volcanic glass, or obsidian.

149

Volcanic rocks

There is fire raging inside the Earth, and this volcanic activity gives birth to interesting rocks. Some of them form deep underground from the unbelievably hot liquid rock called magma. The rest form at the surface, when equally hot lava blasts from volcanoes.

Pumice
This rock is made from fizzy, frothy lava. It is full of holes made by gas bubbles, so it feels rough and is extremely light. It is the only rock that floats.

Pele's hair
Sometimes strings of lava are thrown out of a volcano and stretch in midair. This fibrous golden rock is the result. It looks like human hair and is named after Hawaii's goddess of volcanoes.

Rhyolite
This unusual pink rock was created when sticky lava cooled down at the Earth's surface. Gray forms also exist. Sometimes there are gems or glittery crystals of minerals in the rock.

Diorite
The light and dark areas in this rock are different minerals. Around 4,000–6,000 years ago, during the Stone Age, people made ax heads out of it. Diorite looks very similar to granite.

Granite
Granite looks spotty because of the various minerals in it. It is hard and long-lasting, so since ancient times it has been a popular rock for building everything from castles to cathedrals.

Basalt
Basalt is a black rock formed from cooled lava. It is one of the most common rocks on Earth and makes up most of the ocean floor. It is also found on the planet Mars.

Pegmatite
Many precious gems can be found in this pretty rock, including green emeralds and yellow and pink topaz. The rock also contains a wide range of minerals that form in large crystals.

Andesite
This dark rock erupts from volcanoes and can build them, too. It is named after the Andes Mountains in South America, where there are many active volcanoes.

Types of rock

We group rocks by how they are created. Igneous rocks are made when hot magma and lava cool down and turn solid. Sedimentary rocks form from layers of material dumped by rivers. Metamorphic rocks were formed by extreme heat or pressure.

Igneous

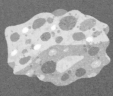

Sedimentary

Metamorphic

151

Volcanic eruption

When a volcano erupts, it belches burning clouds of smoke, ash, and toxic gas and shoots rock bombs high into the air. Rivers of red-hot lava pour down the sides of the volcano. As air or water cools the surface of the lava, it forms a dark crust of volcanic rock.

Rainbow wood is another name for these bright fossils.

Turned to stone
It took many thousands of years to petrify this wood. Water mixed with minerals trickled through the log, leaving behind tiny crystals as it passed.

The growth rings are still visible in the fossilized wood.

A layer of petrified bark can be seen around the outside of the trunk.

Growth rings
Tree trunks have rings of light and dark wood inside them. The dark wood usually grows in the winter, so the number of rings can help tell you how old the tree is.

Petrified wood

Sometimes ancient wood turns into stone, filled with brilliant colors.

The word petrified means "turned to stone," and this circular rock was once part of a living tree growing in a forest about 225 million years ago. When the tree died, its trunk fell to the ground and was covered over by thick, soggy mud. Dead wood normally rots away and turns into splinters and dust. However, this log was protected by the mud and so did not break apart and disappear. Instead, ever so gradually, the wood was replaced by colorful minerals until eventually the log had become solid rock!

This slice of trunk belonged to an araucaria tree, and it was found in Southwestern United States. Here, an entire forest was petrified—along with a lot of other plants and animals. The forest was alive in the Earth's distant past, during a span of time called the Triassic Period, which was when the first dinosaurs appeared. Back then, all of today's continents were bunched together into a single enormous piece of land called Pangea, and the ground was mostly covered in thick woodlands of tall conifer trees just like this one.

Araucaria
(Araucarioxylon)
This tree was an evergreen conifer that grew to around 200 ft (60 m) tall. Its modern relatives live mostly in Oceania and South America.

Mineral colors
Petrified wood is much more colorful than living wood. Its incredible colors come from the different minerals that formed sparkling crystals when the wood was turning into stone. Each crystal color is linked to a particular mineral or substance inside it.

Iron

Iron, Uranium

Chromium, Copper, Iron

Copper, Iron

Quartz

Carbon, Manganese

155

Ammonite
(Speetoniceras)
This ammonite lived around 120 million years ago. Ammonites swam in the sea and used their tentacles to grab food.

Fossil

A seashell made of solid rock can tell us what life was like millions of years ago.

Although it might look like any shell lying on a sandy beach today, this beautiful spiral belonged to an ammonite—an ancient relative of today's squid and octopuses. Millions of years ago, the ocean was home to many kinds of ammonite. Up on the land, the world was ruled by giant dinosaurs and the skies were filled not with birds but with flying reptiles called pterosaurs. All of these animals have now gone. They became extinct about 66 million years ago, never to be seen alive again. So how do we know they existed?

Everything we know about ammonites and other kinds of prehistoric life comes from fossils, like this one. A fossil is anything that remains from a long-dead life-form. Generally, it is the hard parts that survive, like bones, shells, or tree trunks. If they were quickly buried, some of these parts gradually turned into stone, perfectly preserving their original shape. Fossil experts, called paleontologists, study fossils to figure out how the animal or plant that made them lived.

How fossils form

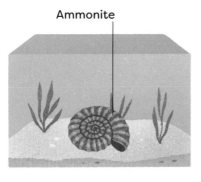

Ammonite

1. When an ammonite died, it sank to the bottom of the ocean. Its soft body parts slowly rotted away, leaving the hard shell behind.

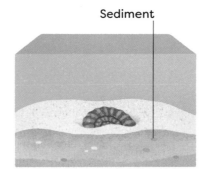

Sediment

2. The shell became buried under sand and mud, or sediment. As more layers were added above, the sediment turned to stone.

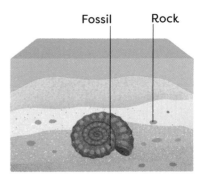

Fossil   Rock

3. Minerals in the sediment formed crystals, which gradually replaced the original materials in the shell. Over millions of years, the shell turned to rock.

Spiral home

The ammonite shell grew in sections, or chambers, with the newest one a bit bigger than the last. The creature lived in the largest chamber at the wide end of the shell.

Many ammonite shells spiral around and around, with bumpy ridges on the surface.

The biggest ammonites grew to 6½ ft (2 m) wide.

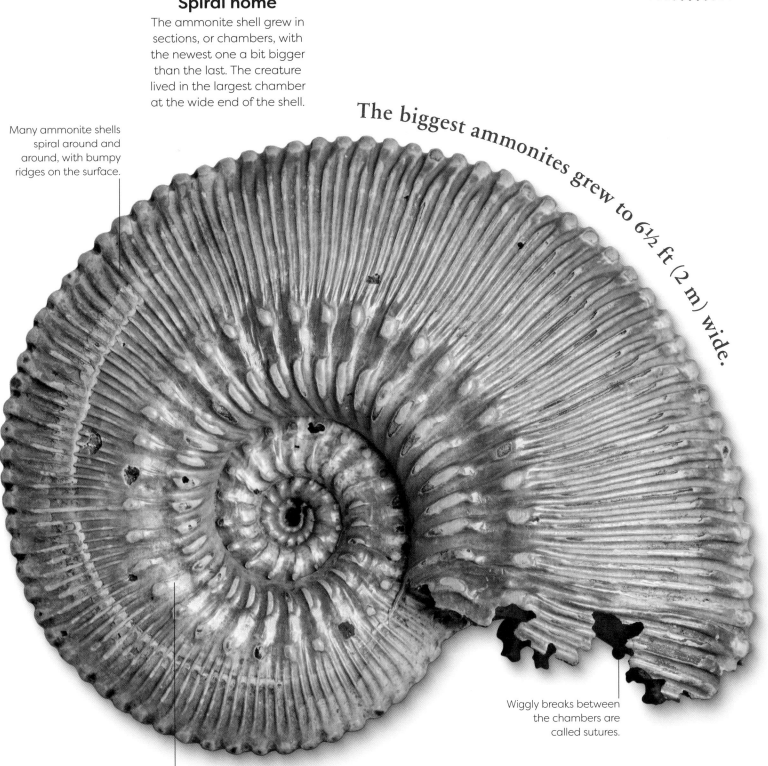

Wiggly breaks between the chambers are called sutures.

The rainbow colors come from minerals in the rocky shell.

Twisting chambers

If an ammonite shell is cut in half, you can see it contained hollow chambers. When alive, water could fill or empty the chambers to help the animal float or sink.

Fossils

Some long-dead plants and animals left behind remains in the ground, called fossils. These are rocky reminders of the ancient life-forms that existed in the distant past. Studying fossils allows us to see back in time to when the living world was very different from how it is now.

Coprolite

This might look like fossilized poop—and that is because it is. The solid stone dung helps us figure out what the animal that made it was eating at the time.

Belemnite

This sharp, tongue-shaped stone is the fossilized inner shell of a squidlike creature called a belemnite. The fossil has turned to opal and shines blue and green.

Crinoid

These ridged tubes are parts of the stems of feathery sea creatures called crinoids, or sea lilies. They are relatives of sea stars and sea urchins, and some still exist today.

Trilobite

This is an early relative of today's insects, crabs, and spiders. Trilobites lived at the bottom of the sea more than 250 million years ago, and there were many kinds.

Iguanodon footprint

This is the footprint of a dinosaur, called an Iguanodon, which stepped in some mud 120 million years ago. The print was preserved and shows fossil experts how the dinosaur walked.

Tree fern frond

Tree ferns look like tall trees with a leafy fern growing from the top. This frond was squished flat by some mud millions of years ago and left a print of its branches and leaves.

Albertosaurus skull

This is a safe way to get a close look at this giant dinosaur. In life, Albertosaurus stood 33 ft (10 m) tall. It used its huge, curved teeth to rip up its prey.

The skull alone is about 3 ft (1 m) long.

Trace fossil

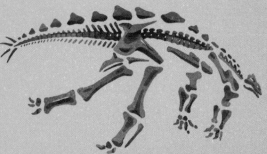

Body fossil

Types of fossil

Fossils are the preserved remains or traces of life from the past. Most fossils are made from hard body parts like bones, wood, and shells. Marks left behind, like a footprint or burrow, are trace fossils.

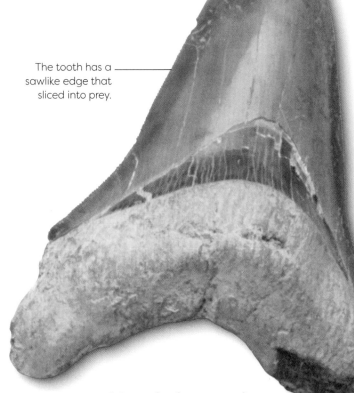

The tooth has a sawlike edge that sliced into prey.

Megalodon tooth

This 7 in (18 cm) tooth belonged to the largest shark that ever lived. Megalodons were 65 ft (20 m) long and hunted whales. They existed around 20 to 4 million years ago.

Fulgurite

When lightning scorches the ground, it can turn sand and stone into twisting sculptures.

Lightning is a type of electricity made in storm clouds, and it is one of many powerful forces that shape the Earth. As a lightning bolt tears through the sky, it superheats the air until it is several times hotter than the surface of the sun. If it strikes a tree, it can boil the water inside, which makes the tree explode. Sometimes lightning sets fire to a grassland or forest, and the resulting blaze may spread for miles. However, every now and again, rather than being destructive, lightning can create an object, known as a fulgurite.

This strange item often looks like a stony tube or branch, and its name comes from the Latin word "fulgur," which means lightning. It forms at the precise spot where the lightning punctured the ground and melted together whatever materials it hit. They say lightning never strikes the same place twice, so if you want to find a fulgurite, how do you know where to look? Sandy beaches and mountains are likely places, but even here you will need lots of luck—fulgurites are very rare indeed.

Lightning

During a lightning strike, a massive electric current flows down to Earth. The air temperature around the lightning bolt may hit 54,000°F (30,000°C)!

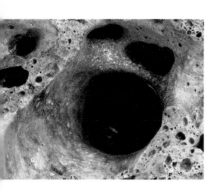

Twisting tunnels

Holes inside a fulgurite show where the lightning entered the ground. Each branch of a lightning bolt creates a tube.

An opening at one end shows where the lightning hit the ground.

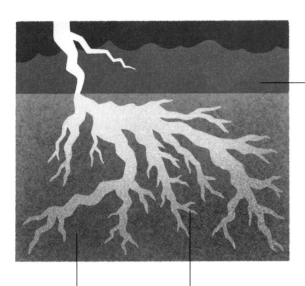

Storm

Sand

Melted glass

Fulgurite formation

Most fulgurites are produced in areas of sand or sandstone. Sand mostly consists of a material called silica. When silica is struck by lightning, it melts into silica glass, which is the main ingredient of fulgurites.

The surface is bumpy and grainy.

The tube is made from melted sand, stones, and other debris.

Odds and ends

Inside, the fulgurite is smooth and glassy, unlike the outside, which feels rough. There is no recipe for fulgurite. It contains whatever materials became mixed with the melted sand.

161

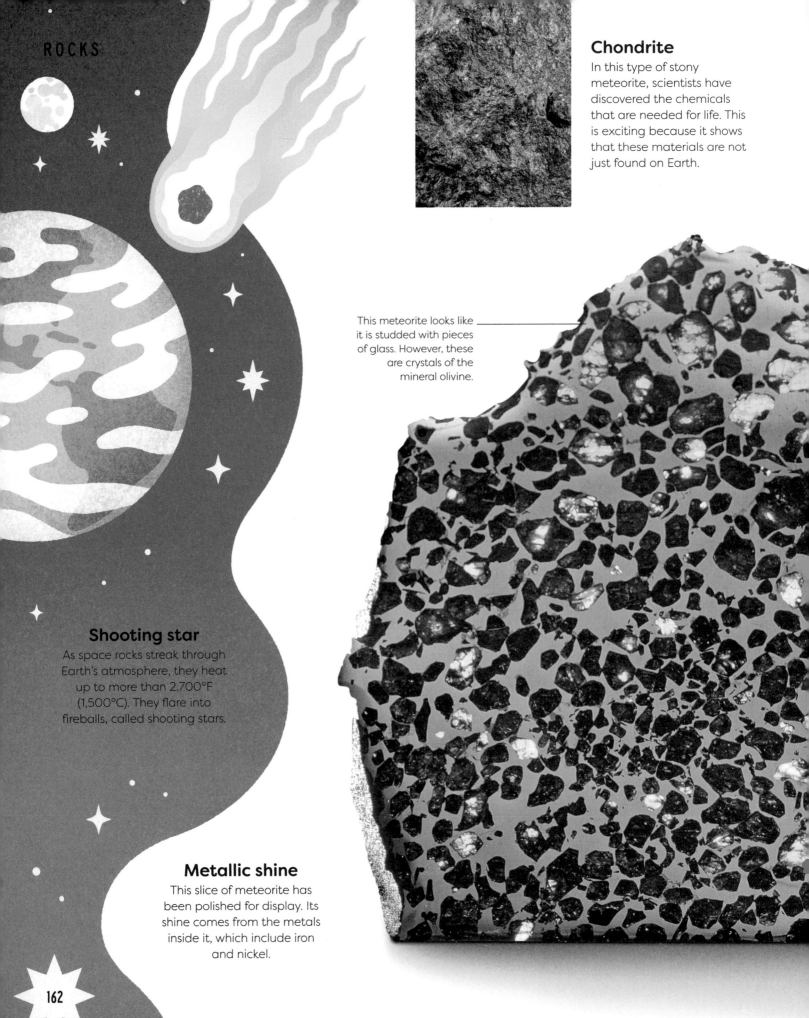

Chondrite

In this type of stony meteorite, scientists have discovered the chemicals that are needed for life. This is exciting because it shows that these materials are not just found on Earth.

This meteorite looks like it is studded with pieces of glass. However, these are crystals of the mineral olivine.

Shooting star

As space rocks streak through Earth's atmosphere, they heat up to more than 2,700°F (1,500°C). They flare into fireballs, called shooting stars.

Metallic shine

This slice of meteorite has been polished for display. Its shine comes from the metals inside it, which include iron and nickel.

Meteorite

These ancient space rocks give us clues about how the Earth formed and life may have begun.

Earth speeds through space at 100,000 ft (30,000 m) every second. As it whizzes along, it hits millions of pieces of floating dust and rock. Almost all this space clutter burns up in the planet's atmosphere, although a few lumps reach ground level. These are meteorites. They are chunks of stone or metal, or a mixture of both. What we find is just the inside, because the outer layer melts as it falls. Usually meteorites weigh less than 2 lb (1 kg). However, bigger ones can make large dents in the ground, called craters, when they land. Luckily, those are rare!

Where do meteorites come from? A handful have arrived from the moon or Mars and the rest from other parts of the solar system. All are incredibly old. Most formed 4.5 billion years ago, together with the Earth, so they can tell us more about what our own world is built from. Meteorites can also contain water and the basic chemicals from which living things are made. Perhaps, like a kind of space delivery service, they brought the essential ingredients that started life on Earth.

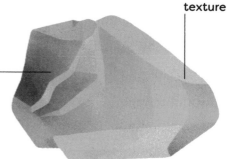

Green color

Glassy texture

Olivine

Ingredients of a meteorite

Olivine is a green mineral often found in meteorites. Many meteorites are full of iron or minerals that contain silicon. Other substances in meteorites include gold, platinum, and all kinds of precious gems, such as diamonds.

CHAPTER 4

Made by nature

Some of the strangest natural objects are not parts of animals or plants, nor are they pieces of minerals. They are items created by animal engineers, such as the nests that are carefully constructed by birds. These objects are made from all kinds of materials. Other unusual items are produced by animals from curious substances, some of which have long been a puzzle to humans.

Honeycomb

Honeybees build slabs of honeycomb with a regular hexagonal pattern.

Honeybee
(Apis mellifera)
Honeybees live worldwide. Wild colonies nest in hollow trees and cracks in rock, while domesticated honeybees inhabit hives built by humans.

Lots of honeybees are buzzing around their nest inside an old apple tree. Already full-size, the colony is home to 50,000 female worker bees, ruled by a single queen. Older workers stream in and out as they head off to visit flowers or return with loads of pollen and nectar. Younger bees stay behind to perform jobs in the nest. One of their most important tasks is building honeycomb, which forms the main structure of their home.

The bees construct row after row of identical tubes, or cells. They sculpt the cell walls out of sticky wax taken from glands near the ends of their bodies. To produce the wax, they gorge on the nest's stored honey. It takes 2 lb (1 kg) of honey to create just 2 oz (55 g) of honeycomb. The cells have a six-sided, or hexagonal, shape that enables them to fit together with no wasted space between them. Each layer of cells backs onto another to create the golden slabs that hang down in the nest. The snug cells are used as both nurseries for baby bees and cupboards for the colony's food.

Inside the nest
In a wild nest, the pieces of honeycomb are often roughly oval. They hang side by side in vertical sheets but don't completely fill the space. This leaves room for air to flow and for bees to move around the nest.

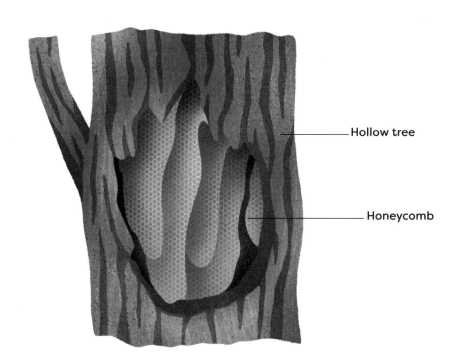

Hollow tree

Honeycomb

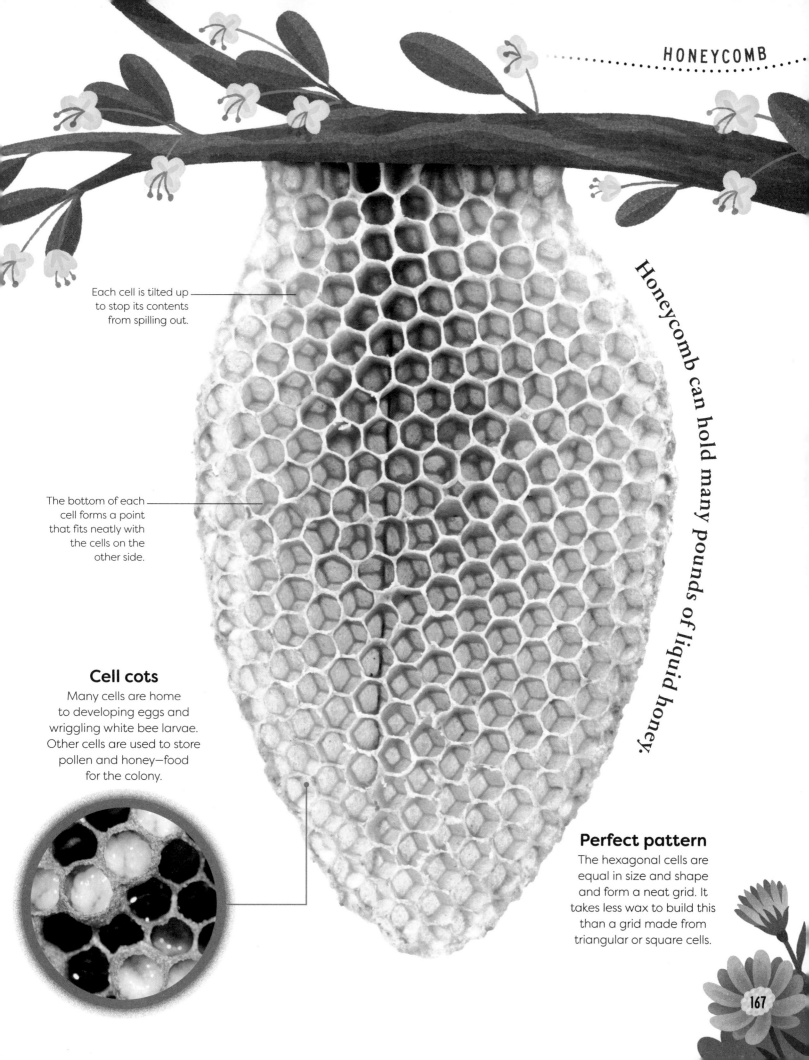

Honeycomb can hold many pounds of liquid honey.

Each cell is tilted up to stop its contents from spilling out.

The bottom of each cell forms a point that fits neatly with the cells on the other side.

Cell cots
Many cells are home to developing eggs and wriggling white bee larvae. Other cells are used to store pollen and honey—food for the colony.

Perfect pattern
The hexagonal cells are equal in size and shape and form a neat grid. It takes less wax to build this than a grid made from triangular or square cells.

167

Gathering material

Moss and grass are the favorite nest materials of chaffinches. Small twigs give strength, feathers offer warmth, and sticky spiders' webs hold everything together.

Different jobs

Chaffinch nests usually take about a week to build, with most construction done by the female. Meanwhile, the male defends their territory.

The inside of the nest is lined with feathers, hair, and dry grass for warmth.

Frilly lichen is added to the outer wall of the nest as camouflage to help hide it in the trees.

A female chaffinch makes around 1,300 trips to fetch nest material.

Songbird nest

A bird's nest is a cleverly engineered home for eggs and chicks.

Imagine building a nest without any hands! This is what birds do with just a bill and feet as their tools. It is an incredible achievement. Songbirds include thousands of species worldwide, from hummingbirds and swallows to robins, finches, and crows, all of which build nests unique to their species. The urge to build is pure instinct, and so is the design of the structure. In other words, a bird hatches with this knowledge already wired into its brain. It doesn't need to be given a plan. However, birds get better with practice and they learn from their mistakes. They adapt their approach if it is not working—for example, by adding more or less of certain materials.

Chaffinches, like many songbirds, create round, cuplike nests, hidden among the leaves of a bush or tree. This will be a safe home for their eggs and chicks as they grow. The female makes the base first, then builds up the sides and weaves in strands of grass to make the shape. To form a perfect cup, she sits in the nest and turns around in a circle.

Common chaffinch
(*Fringilla coelebs*)
Chaffinches are often seen in gardens, parks, and woods, all across Europe and western Asia. Males have an orange face and belly, while females are brown.

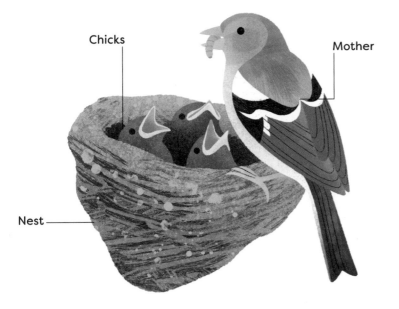

Chicks

Mother

Nest

Temporary home
A female chaffinch lays four or five eggs in a nest and incubates them for 12 days. Only she feeds the chicks, bringing them juicy caterpillars up to eight times an hour. Within 16 days of hatching, the chicks leave, and the nest is never used again.

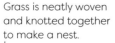

A narrow entrance slit
is found on one side.

Red ovenbird

Argentina's national bird makes
a ball-shaped nest from clay or
mud, which becomes rock-hard in
the sun. Its shape resembles that of
traditional wood-fired clay ovens.

Grass is neatly woven
and knotted together
to make a nest.

Southern masked weaver

Male southern masked weavers
weave grass into tubes or globes,
with a nesting chamber hidden inside.
The nests are hung from the tips of
thin, flexible branches so predators
can't get in.

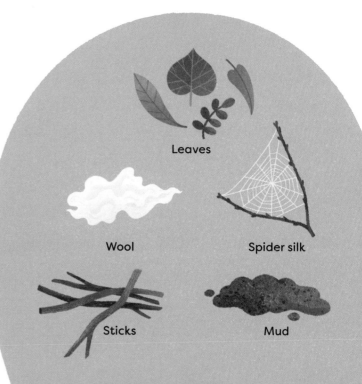

Leaves

Wool

Spider silk

Sticks

Mud

Building materials

Birds usually use whatever natural materials are
most plentiful in their habitat, such as moss, grass,
and feathers, to build a nest. Some items are chosen
for their shape or strength, while others provide
warmth or can be used as glue. Many nests will
contain several types of material.

Bird nests

Birds are impressive architects that build nests for their growing young from almost anything, including saliva and mud! Some use these materials in ingenious ways. For example, blue tits add strong-smelling leaves that stop bacteria from growing, while European starlings add herbs that act as insect repellent.

Long-tailed tit

This ball-shaped nest is amazingly stretchy because it contains so much soft moss and spider silk. The nest is able to expand as the fast-growing young get larger.

Cave swiftlet

Several swifts mix their own saliva into their nests, but this species uses nothing else! It sticks its nest high up on the walls of caves in rain forests in Southeast Asia.

Reed warbler

These secretive warblers live in marshes in dense forests of reeds. They sling their nest between several reed stems so that it hangs over the water of the marsh.

Osprey

Birds of prey, such as ospreys, build a huge, messy platform of sticks. Since breeding pairs stay together for life, the nest is reused and added to each year.

Song thrush

This common thrush adds a beautifully smooth lining of mud to its nest. The mud cup is molded by the female as she sits in the nest.

House martin

House martins construct a deep nest under the roofs of buildings. It contains over 1,000 beakfuls of soft wet mud, which hardens like cement as it dries.

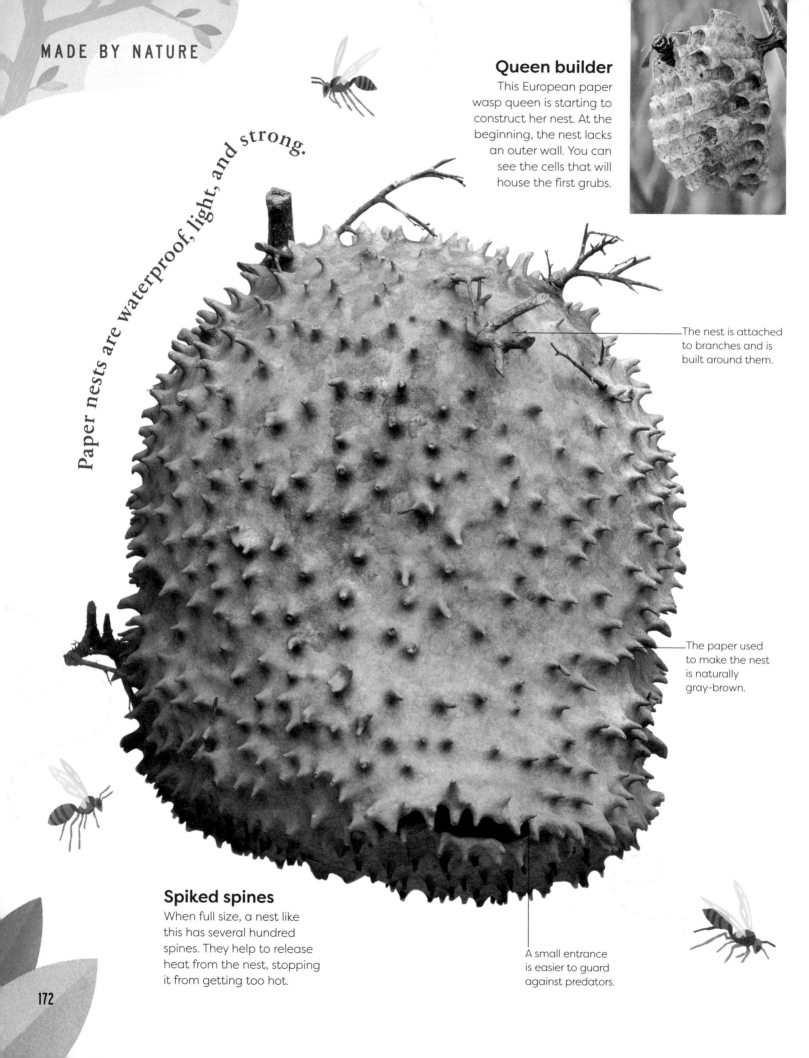

Paper nests are waterproof, light, and strong.

Queen builder
This European paper wasp queen is starting to construct her nest. At the beginning, the nest lacks an outer wall. You can see the cells that will house the first grubs.

The nest is attached to branches and is built around them.

The paper used to make the nest is naturally gray-brown.

Spiked spines
When full size, a nest like this has several hundred spines. They help to release heat from the nest, stopping it from getting too hot.

A small entrance is easier to guard against predators.

Paper wasp nest

Paper wasps are social insects that create paper palaces and extend them as their colonies grow.

Working as a team, paper wasps are able to build nests that compared to them are enormous. The queen wasp starts the construction process alone, and then her many daughters, or workers, take over. They use nothing but paper. To make the nest, they use their scissorlike jaws to slice off strips of wood to chew—you can hear them as they work. The wood is mixed in with saliva to form a wet pulp, which hardens as it dries. Their lovely paper nest is a nursery, food pantry, and fortress all in one. Every species of paper wasp has its own design of nest. Common shapes include cylinders, spheres, ovals, bells, or upside-down pyramids. Often their surface looks like swirls of meringue, although a few are smooth or have sharp spines. As more wasps hatch, the nests keep expanding, until they are a base for as many as 30,000 buzzing workers. It is said that around 2,100 years ago, a Chinese government official was watching wasps make nests like these and had the brilliant idea for paper. It is one of the most useful inventions ever!

Paper wasp
(Polybia scutellaris)
There are many kinds of paper wasp. This species from South America builds a spiked nest and even fills it with honey.

Inside the nest

A nest has hundreds or thousands of hexagonal cells. Each is a home for an egg or grub. The cells are created in layers, stacked like the floors of a multistory building. Due to the nest's clever structure, its temperature never changes.

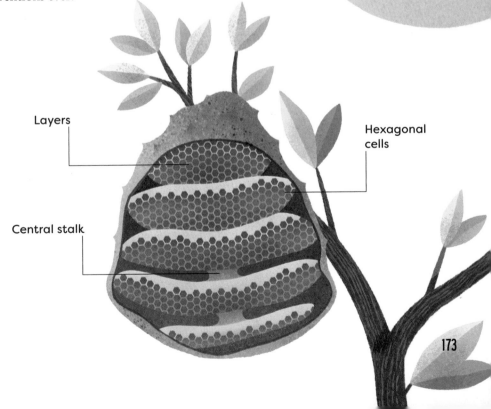

Layers

Hexagonal cells

Central stalk

173

Potter wasp
(Eumeninae)
People need not fear
these attractive little wasps,
which rarely sting. They live
throughout the northern
half of the world.

Potter wasp pot

The female potter wasp crafts mud into a clay nursery for her young.

Many wasps build nests out of paper made from wood pulp, but this requires a large workforce containing lots of individuals. Wasps that live alone need a different plan. A female potter wasp is able to construct nurseries single-handedly, using clay from a nearby puddle or riverbank. She flies back and forth to carry it to a tree or rock, where she carefully creates a structure shaped like a pot or vase. Compared to wasps that make paper nests, her jaws are long and narrow—a shape that is better for sculpting the clay. As the clay dries, the pot becomes rock-hard, which is perfect for keeping out predators and the weather. The mother wasp lays an egg inside the nursery and then seals it shut. What will the young wasp eat when it hatches? The attentive mother wasp has already stored juicy caterpillars inside the pot as a ready-made snack!

Wasps are not the only insects that make nurseries from clay. Antlike termites construct massive mounds as tall as three-story houses in the tropical grasslands of Africa, Oceania, and South America. Only determined predators can break into these clay fortresses.

Inside the pot

In the finished pot, the egg hatches into a grublike larva. Also inside the chamber is a paralyzed caterpillar, or sometimes several, for the larva to dine on. Safe from harm, the wasp larva feeds day and night, so it grows rapidly.

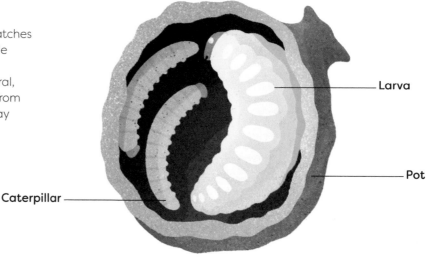

Larva

Pot

Caterpillar

Potter wasps are extremely fussy about the clay that they use.

Each nest has rounded walls, with a wide base and narrow neck.

Sculpting clay
Soft clay is easy to collect and shape. If it is too dry, the wasp moistens it with her own saliva.

Eaten alive
Potter wasp venom immobilizes, or paralyzes, caterpillars, rather than killing them. This way, the wasp larva will have fresh meat to eat.

The mother wasp seals the pot with a blob of clay. When grown, the larva inside must break out.

Every piece of the case is placed with the skill of a bricklayer.

Many materials

Some species of caddisfly are more fussy than others about what they build with. This larva has used leaves to make its home.

Empty water snail shells can be recycled to make part of the case.

A selection of seeds helps make the case tough.

Hollow tube

The hollow case is tiny—only an inch or so long—and it is as fat as a pencil. There is a hidden entrance at one end.

Caddisfly case

Bit by bit, caddisfly larvae build elegant shelters from materials they find in their freshwater habitats.

The larvae, or young, of caddisflies are like weird underwater caterpillars, and probably would not be described as pretty. Yet they live in the most beautiful homes. You will find them at the bottom of clean rivers, streams, and ponds. Here, these insect architects hunt for items such as grains of sand and tiny pieces of leaf or twig. They assemble the materials around their bodies until they end up with a structure like a lumpy sleeping bag. The larvae produce sticky silk to hold everything together. Some make their cases entirely of silk. Most of these shelters are mobile homes that the larvae carry as they walk around. Why go to all this bother? The cases offer protection from hungry fish, and in streams they act as armor against the battering current.

The building work never stops. Cases need constant repair, and when a larva outgrows its case, it needs to move into something larger. Usually it gets through five homes in one or two years, before it is finally ready to leave the water for good and turn into an adult caddisfly.

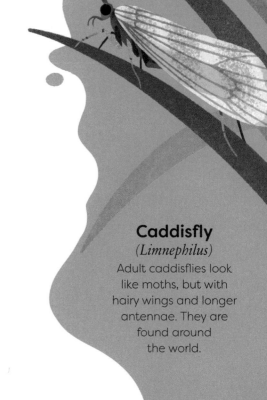

Caddisfly
(Limnephilus)
Adult caddisflies look like moths, but with hairy wings and longer antennae. They are found around the world.

Case

Shells

Larva

Life of a larva
The larva's legs are just behind its head, with its long body hidden in its case. It reaches out of its case to gather food and fresh building material, and to drag itself around. Claws at its rear grip the inside of the case.

Prize possession

Fresh dung is wet and smelly, so it is easy to find. These dung beetles are quick to grab their piece of elephant poop and roll it away before another beetle steals it.

Dung can contain seeds, which the beetles help to spread.

The dung is neatly rolled into a ball.

Dinnertime

Solid parts of the dung are munched by the dung beetle's larvae. Adult beetles slurp the dung's foul liquid like a protein shake!

Pieces of undigested plant can still be seen in the dung.

Dung beetle ball

Neatly rolled packages of poop make the perfect beetle takeout.

Were it not for dung beetles, the world would be swamped in the stinky stuff animals leave behind. They feed on the waste of many creatures, including birds, reptiles, and snails. However, most prefer the poop of grazing animals. Because grassland herbivores generally only half-digest what they eat, their dung still has plenty of nutrients in it. Within minutes of being dumped, a smelly pile attracts dung beetles, which break it up to create food stores for themselves or their larvae. A few species of dung beetle expertly mold the dung into balls, which is the best shape to roll away and bury underground. These beetles are amazingly strong—the horned dung beetle can push a ball more than 1,000 times heavier than itself!

Dung beetles can roll their mucky spheres in a straight line, despite not being able to see where they are going. It is an incredible feat for an insect with a brain the size of a grain of sand. The beetles manage it because they can navigate by the position of the sun, moon, and stars.

Flightless dung beetle
(Circellium bacchus)
This large dung beetle from South Africa can reach 2 in (5 cm) long. It is attracted to the large piles of dung made by elephants.

On the ball
A dung beetle uses its front legs to lift itself off the ground and walk steadily backward. Meanwhile, the second and third pairs of legs grasp the dung ball and roll it carefully along.

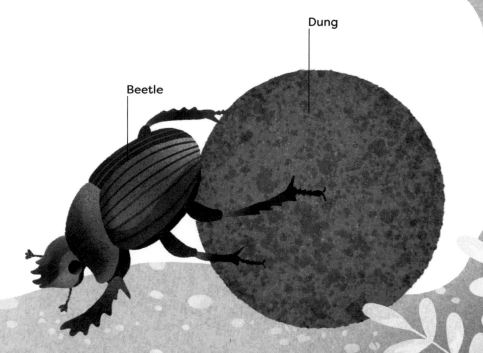

Dung

Beetle

Owl pellet

Anything an owl can't digest, it vomits up as slimy pellets.

Owls, like all birds, can't chew. It is one of the disadvantages of not having jaws lined with teeth. So owls swallow their prey whole, by throwing their heads back to gulp it down headfirst. This may look uncomfortable to us but it works well. There is a problem, though. Few animals—owls included—are able to digest bone, teeth, or fur. Somehow, they must get rid of these indigestible parts of their meal. Owls do it with pellets.

Every owl vomits up balls, called pellets, of the inedible parts of their food. They usually do this on a daily basis. Most pellets drop into the grass or undergrowth and are lost. Barn owl pellets, however, are easier to find because these rodent hunters nest close to humans. They like barns and empty buildings, as well as the nest boxes people put up for them. Searching the floor near a nest may reveal piles of pellets. They are firm and black when fresh, then turn gray and powdery, like ash. Barn owls produce normal droppings, too, but these are chalky white so are easy to tell apart.

Barn owl
(Tyto alba)
The barn owl can be glimpsed on every continent except Antarctica. It has a heart-shaped face and ghostly pale feathers.

Bringing up pellets

A barn owl brings up one or two pellets after a successful night's hunting. The pellets spend around six hours in the owl's digestive system before it coughs them up. It does this while sitting on a favorite perch.

Owl

Pellet

Bundle of bones

Rodent bones in pellets can often be identified, from skulls to backbones. These bones can be teased out, and they tell us which animals were in the owl's last meal.

Fresh barn owl pellets are dark in color.

The bones in the pellet are mostly intact and undamaged.

Careful detective work reveals what the owl ate.

Hairball

Barn owls eat mice and voles. Most of their pellets are made up of fur from their meals, which binds each pellet into a tight bundle.

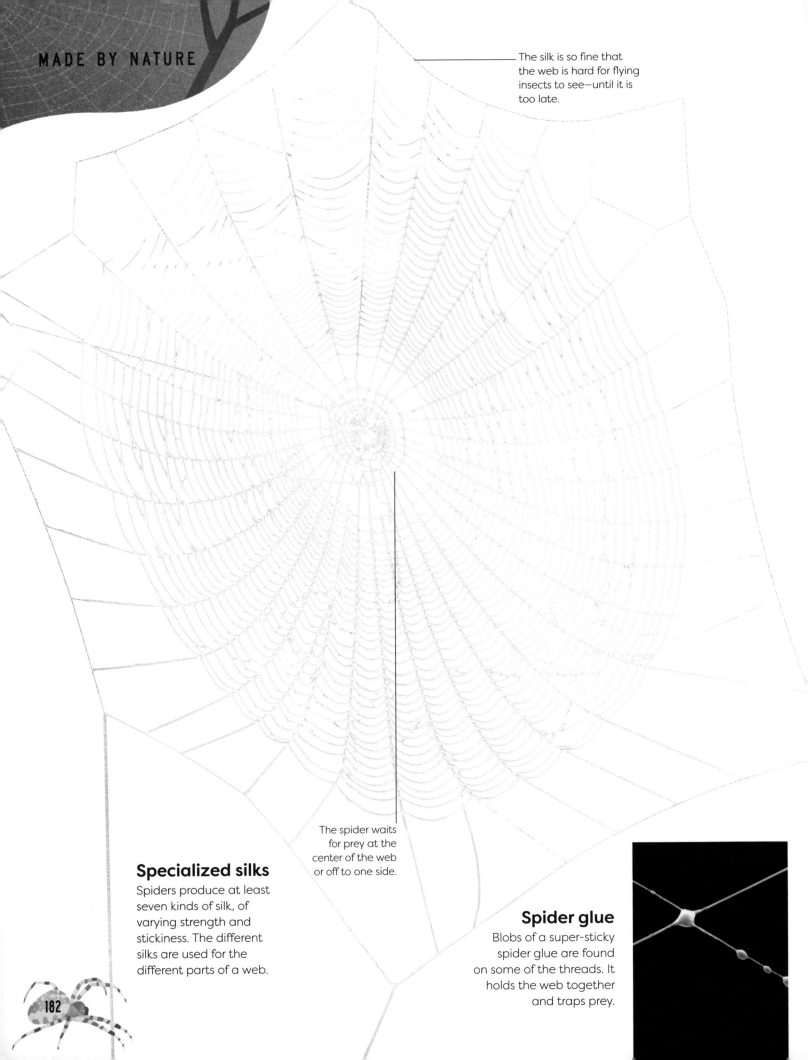

The silk is so fine that the web is hard for flying insects to see—until it is too late.

The spider waits for prey at the center of the web or off to one side.

Specialized silks

Spiders produce at least seven kinds of silk, of varying strength and stickiness. The different silks are used for the different parts of a web.

Spider glue

Blobs of a super-sticky spider glue are found on some of the threads. It holds the web together and traps prey.

182

Spider web

Using its own silk, a spider spins complex webs to trap its insect prey.

Strong and stretchy is a useful combination that is found in everything from rubber bands to bungee cords. Probably the strongest and stretchiest material in the natural world is spider silk. This fiber is so fine it weighs almost nothing, yet it is five times stronger than the same weight of steel. Spiders make it with pointed organs, called spinnerets, at the ends of their bodies. At first, the silk is liquid, but as spiders pull it from the spinnerets using their legs, it sets to form extremely tough threads.

The ultimate webs are created by orb-weaver spiders—such as the garden spider—which spin large, circular nets. Most are made by big females, which need to feed well to produce eggs. Each female spins a fresh web every morning, in under 30 minutes! Her aim is to catch flying insects, which zoom into the web and become stuck in the sticky mesh. As soon as prey hits the web, she pounces. The silk is too precious to waste, so at the end of the day, she recycles the web by eating it.

Garden spider
(Araneus diadematus)
This spider can be seen spinning its webs in gardens, parks, and grassy places across Europe and North America.

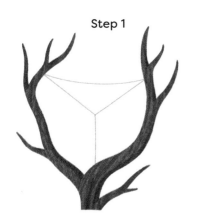
Step 1

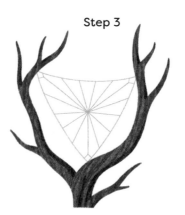
Step 2

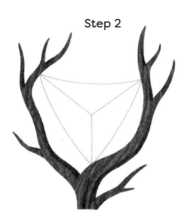
Step 3

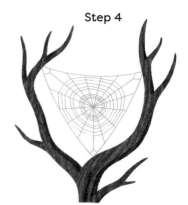
Step 4

Spinning a web

First, a female garden spider secures a line of thread across a gap, then she adds more threads to form a triangle. Next, she creates the spokes of the web, which are finally connected by spirals of her stickiest silk.

Ambergris

Once known as marine gold, this peculiar lumpy substance is made by sperm whales.

What appears to be a stone is lying on a beach, but some things about it are odd. It feels too light to be stone. Stranger still is the smell, with hints of wet woodland, barnyard, and ocean spray. This is actually a piece of sperm whale ambergris. For centuries, its origins were a puzzle. Some people decided it was sea foam turned solid or dragon spit, and others thought it might be a kind of marine fungus. Since then, we have figured out that ambergris is produced by sperm whales.

Sperm whales eat lots of squid, but they are unable to digest the hard squid beaks and internal shells, called pens. Sometimes these tough bits get stuck in a whale's intestines. The whale makes a waxy substance that binds the sharp squid parts together, and, over time, they grow into solid lumps. The lumps pass out of the whale's body like poop, and the ambergris floats free. Because its aroma is so unusual, ambergris has always been worth a fortune. It was particularly valuable in the perfume industry because it helps scent stay on the skin for longer.

On the beach

Ambergris washes up on beaches all over the world. Usually, it is found by dogs because they can smell its strong odor.

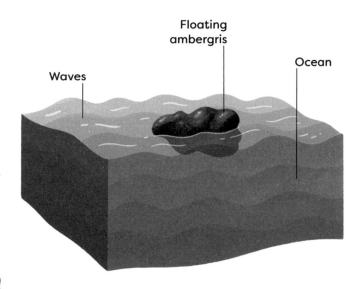

Waves

Floating ambergris

Ocean

On the ocean

When ambergris leaves the whale's body, it is soft and black. It can float on the surface of the ocean for several months or years. The bright sunlight and salty seawater slowly harden it and turn it pale brown, gray, or white.

The surface of ambergris is crusty and waxy.

Sperm whale
(Physeter macrocephalus)
These sleek giants are the world's largest whales with teeth. They hunt squid and fish across the planet, often at great depths.

Pieces of sweet-smelling ambergris are found very rarely.

Powdery surface
If a chunk of ambergris has been in the sea for a long time, its surface may develop powdery white patches.

The hard remains of the sperm whale's food may stay stuck in the ambergris.

185

Glossary

alga organism that mostly lives in water and makes food using the energy from sunlight by photosynthesis. Seaweeds are algae

amphibian animal with thin, often slimy skin that can live in water and on land. Frogs, toads, and newts are examples of amphibians

animal organism that fuels itself by consuming food and reproduces by laying eggs or giving birth to live young. Most animals can move by walking, creeping, swimming, or flying. Invertebrates, fish, amphibians, reptiles, birds, and mammals are animals

arthropod type of invertebrate with a hard, jointed exoskeleton. Insects, crabs, and spiders are arthropods

bark covering of trees that protects the soft wood underneath

bird animal with feathers and a beak that reproduces by laying hard-shelled eggs. Owls, eagles, ducks, and parrots are all examples of birds

bivalve type of mollusk with two shells, or valves, that are connected by a hinge. Scallops, clams, mussels, and oysters are examples of bivalves

bone rigid structure that supports part of a vertebrate's body. Many bones connect together to form the skeleton

calcium carbonate substance made from calcium, carbon, and oxygen that makes up the rock chalk. It is also found in bones and shells

camouflage apperance of an organism that helps it hide in its surroundings

canine type of pointed tooth found near the front of a mammal's jaws. Carnivores usually have large canine teeth for gripping prey

carbohydrate type of substance made by living organisms. Sugars and starch are carbohydrates. Potatoes and grains contain lots of carbohydrate

carnivore organism that eats meat

cellulose tough material found in plants

cephalopod type of mollusk that feeds with tentacles. Octopuses and squid are examples of cephalopods

chitin tough material found in arthropods and fungi. It gives strength to insect exoskeletons

clutch group of eggs laid by a single animal

colony big group of animals that all live together, often in the same home, such as bees and wasps

crustacean type of arthropod with antennae, many legs, and a tough exoskeleton. Crabs, shrimp, and lobsters are examples of crustaceans

crystal type of mineral form that usually has a geometric shape with many flat sides and straight edges

deciduous description of trees that lose all their leaves once a year and then regrow them

egg cell from which a baby animal grows. Outside, eggs can be soft, as in amphibians; leathery, as in reptiles; or hard, as in birds

element simplest form of a chemical, which can't be broken down further

embryo young organism at an early stage of development found inside a seed, an egg, or a womb

enamel hard material covering teeth

evergreen description of trees that have leaves all year round

extinct when there are none of a particular species left alive

exoskeleton hard covering that supports the body of some creatures. Exoskeletons must be molted for the animal to grow bigger

fish animal with fins and scales that lives underwater. Salmon, eels, and sharks are examples of fish

fossil rock that is the preserved remains or traces of an organism that lived many years ago

fossilization process by which an organism turns to rock over many years. Usually only hard parts of a life-form become fossilized. For example, bones, shells, and branches

fruit structure that surrounds a plant's seeds. Fruits can be fleshy, such as an apple, or dry, such as a maple key

fungus organism that usually grows in soil and gets its food by digesting the remains of plants and animals. Mushrooms, toadstools, and molds are parts of fungi

gastropod type of mollusk that crawls on a strong, muscular foot. Slugs and snails are examples of gastropods

gemstone mineral that is colorful or rare and used in jewelry

gill feathery organ that some animals use to breathe underwater

habitat place where an organism lives. Certain life-forms can only survive in specific habitats. For example, an ocean, rain forest, or desert

herbivore organism that eats plants

host organism that another type of organism benefits from. For example, dogs are hosts of fleas, which suck their blood, and other birds are the hosts of cuckoos, which lay their eggs in the host's nest

incisor type of tooth found in mammals at the very front of the mouth. The incisors of elephants have become tusks

incubation process of keeping an egg warm so the baby inside can grow. Birds usually sit on their eggs to incubate them, and reptiles often bury their eggs in warm sand or rotting vegetation

invertebrate animal with no backbone. Some invertebrates have other internal or external skeletons that support their bodies. Worms, insects, and mollusks are examples of invertebrates

keratin tough material found in some animals. Keratin makes up hair, nails, claws, feathers, and horns

larva young of certain animals, including insects and amphibians. Larvae can look very different from the adult creature

lignin tough material found in plants

mammal animal with hair that usually gives birth to its young. Deer, elephants, whales, camels, and rodents are all examples of mammals

metamorphosis process by which certain animals including insects and amphibians transform from a larva to an adult

migration process by which certain animals travel a long distance from one place to another, usually to breed or find food

mineral substance made from a specific mixture of elements. Minerals always have crystals and can be brightly colored

molar type of tooth found in mammals. Herbivores usually have large, flat molars to grind up plants

mollusk type of invertebrate animal with a soft body and often a shell, such as slugs and snails, octopuses and squid, and bivalves

molting process of shedding body coverings, which are then replaced. Birds molt their feathers and insects molt their exoskeletons

muscle strong organ that animals use to help them move. Muscles can shorten or lengthen to pull body parts into different positions

nacre hard material made by some bivalves to coat the inside of their shells. Nacre is made from calcium carbonate

nectar sweet liquid made by plants to attract pollinators

nest structure built by an animal in which to raise its young

nymph type of larva that changes gradually from a baby to an adult

parasite organism that benefits from another organism. Many parasites live on or inside a host's body or in its home and steal its nutrients

photosynthesis process by which plants make sugar using the energy from sunlight

pigment colorful substance. For example, the pigment chlorophyll makes leaves green

plant organism that usually grows in soil and makes food from sunlight by photosynthesis. Trees, shrubs, and flowers are plants

poisonous description of an organism that makes poison. Poisons are toxic substances that will kill or damage an organism that eats or touches them

pollen minute grains produced by male flowers or cones in order for the plant to reproduce

pollinator animal that transfers pollen from the male parts of a flower to the female parts

predator animal that hunts and kills other animals, called prey, for food

prey animal that is hunted and killed by other animals, called predators

protein type of substance made by living organisms. For example, muscles are mainly made of proteins

reptile animal with scales that breathes air. Snakes, lizards, crocodiles, and turtles are examples of reptiles

rock substance made from a mixture of minerals. Rocks are usually hard and they make up the Earth's outer layer

scale small, tough plate that protects the bodies of some animals. Reptiles and fish are completely covered in scales

seed structure produced by plants from which a new plant grows

seed head structure produced by a plant that contains and protects its seeds

shell hard, protective covering. Animal shells are usually made of calcium carbonate. Some plants produce nuts with shells made of cellulose and lignin

skeleton internal or external framework that supports an animal's body. In vertebrates, the skeleton is made of many bones or cartilage

solar system area in space containing the sun and the planets that orbit it, including the Earth

species type of organism. Members of the same species can breed together and usually look similar

spore dustlike grains similar to seeds that mosses, ferns, and fungi use to reproduce

tentacle long limb of certain animals used to grab food. Corals, octopuses, and squid have tentacles

venomous description of an organism that makes venom. Venoms are toxic substances that will kill or damage an organism injected with them

vertebrate animal that has a backbone as part of its internal skeleton. Fish, amphibians, reptiles, birds, and mammals are examples of vertebrates

volcano place where lava erupts from inside the Earth. Many volcanoes are cone-shaped

Index

DK | Penguin Random House

Author Ben Hoare
Illustrator Kaley McKean

Project Editor Olivia Stanford
Designer Sonny Flynn
US Editor Margaret Parrish
US Senior Editor Shannon Beatty
Publishing Coordinator Issy Walsh
Project Art Editor Kanika Kalra
Senior Production Editor Rob Dunn
Senior Production Controller Francesca Sturiale
Project Picture Researcher Vagisha Pushp
DTP Designers Sachin Gupta, Syed Md Farhan
Managing Editor Jonathan Melmoth
Managing Art Editors Diane Peyton Jones,
Ivy Sengupta
Deputy Art Director Mabel Chan
Publishing Director Sarah Larter

Additional text Tom Jackson
Biology Consultant Dr. Amy-Jane Beer
Minerals Consultant Dr. Devin Dennie

First American Edition, 2021
Published in the United States by DK Publishing
1450 Broadway, Suite 801, New York, NY 10018

Text copyright © Ben Hoare 2021
Copyright © 2021 Dorling Kindersley Limited
DK, a Division of Penguin Random House LLC
21 22 23 24 25 10 9 8 7 6 5 4 3 2 1
001–319091–Nov/2021

A catalog record for this book
is available from the Library of Congress.
ISBN 978-0-7440-3495-0

DK books are available at special discounts when purchased
in bulk for sales promotions, premiums, fund-raising, or educational use. For
details, contact: DK Publishing Special Markets,
1450 Broadway, Suite 801, New York, NY 10018
SpecialSales@dk.com

Printed and bound in China

For the curious

www.dk.com

DK would like to thank: Sally Beets, Marie Greenwood, Kieran Jones, Katie Lawrence, Manisha Majithia, Niharika Prabhakar, and Kathleen Teece for editorial assistance; Debra Wolter for proofreading; and Helen Peters for the index.